NORMAN J. COLE IN

by Norman J. Cole

1st Edition 2007

ISBN 978-0-9556229-0-8

Published by Geoff J. Cole

Printed by Uniprint Limited 020 8673 8736

Images on pages 3, 198 & 199 are Marks of the Secretary of State
for Defence and are reproduced with their permission

I dedicate these memoirs
to my wonderful family
and to the unknown soldier.*

*In the First World War my father was a soldier in the Royal
Fusiliers. During the battle of the Somme, he was seriously wounded
and left for dead on the battlefield. A passing soldier noticed a small
movement, picked my father up and carried him back for medical
treatment. But for the compassion of that unknown soldier, I, and
therefore my family, would not exist.

About the Author

Norman Cole was born in Torquay in 1922, the only child of William James Cole and Freda Annie Cole. At the age of five he became a pupil of the Chelston and Cockington School. In 1933 he took the 11+ examination, (to determine which Senior School he would attend) and after passing, started at the Homelands Central School.

On leaving school, although his parents could not afford the normal premium, he was appointed as a trainee by a Chartered Accountant, and was paid two shillings and sixpence as pocket money. This Accountant was an Australian and decided to return to his native land but, before doing so, obtained a job for Norman with a local building firm as an office boy. Whilst working in the builder's office, he undertook an evening course in building construction. Having obtained certificates in the related subjects, he was transferred to the surveying section of the firm and worked in that capacity until his recruitment into the forces.

In 1942 he was called to the army and the details are incorporated in these memoirs.

At the end of World War II, his pre-war employer applied for his early release to allow him to take responsibility for a large housing contract in Torquay; this was approved. Thus ended his army career.

His varied appointments thereafter were as follows:-

Surveyor with British Railway (Eastern Region).

Manager of a Quantity Surveyor's office in Barnstaple, Devon.

Senior Quantity Surveyor with Cheltenham Borough Council.

Deputy Chief Quantity Surveyor with Plymouth Corporation.

Principal Quantity Surveyor with Hemel Hempstead Development Corporation.

Principal of his own QS. practice in Hemel Hempstead.

Cost Controller and Chief Quantity Surveyor with the London Borough of Harrow, and finally

Principal Quantity Surveyor with Devon County Council, taking early retirement in 1984.

During his time at Harrow he was appointed as consultant to a Government seminar (re Third London Airport).

He was a member of a small team which led to the formation of the Society of Chief Quantity Surveyors and was appointed Membership Secretary with delegated authority to accept or reject applications for membership.

Part time professional appointments

Lecturer at the Plymouth Technical College, covering examination courses including Building Estimating, Building Site Organisation and Records, etc.

Consultant Principal Lecturer at Hatfield Polytechnic, Hertfordshire, in Post Graduate study of Civil Engineering Contracts and in the Law of Arbitration.

His professional qualifications

Fellow of the Royal Institution of Chartered Surveyors.

Fellow of the Chartered Institute of Arbitrators.

His non-work activities have included the following

Charter Member of the Hemel Hempstead Lions Club, then Lions Clubs Zone Chairman (Responsible for five clubs), and then Deputy District Governor (with responsibility for clubs in London and the South East of England).

Treasurer of the League of Friends of the Starcross and Langdon Psychiatric Hospitals, in South Devon.

Formed two Boys' Brigade Companies and became their Captain, one in Barnstaple, Devon, and the other in Hemel Hempstead, Hertfordshire.

Co-opted to the committee of the Boys' Brigade Felden Lodge Training Centre as consultant Surveyor.

An Elder of Teignmouth Baptist Church for over twenty years.

Norman's immediate family details

Wife - Kathleen Mary Elizabeth (nee McBrearty).

Children - Geoffrey, Ruth and Richard.

Grandchildren - Gregory, Kevin, Kathryn, Julia, Jenny and Vicky.

Contents

Foreword by Peter Hart

It is a pleasure to write a preface for this excellent book by Norman Cole. In my work at the Imperial War Museum Sound Archive I get to meet a lot of 'ordinary men' who served their country with distinction in the Second World War. But when you actually meet a man like Norman, you suddenly realise that 'ordinary' is a much-abused word. If he had not been born in 1922 then he would probably have led a quiet life as a building surveyor in his native Devon. But, like so many men of his generation, he was caught up in global conflict. Initially his was a reserved occupation, so he worked hard in providing splinter proof skins around the Torpoint oil tanks.

When he joined the Army, his specialist skills led him to the Royal Artillery School of Survey at Larkhill in 1942. Here he learnt the arcane skills of sound ranging and flash spotting. From then on Norman would fight his war using his brain, not brawn - although as he was also later trained in 'silent killing methods', such a distinction can be over-stated! Once trained, he served with the 9th Survey Regt., RA and would ultimately land on Sword Beach during the D-Day invasion of Normandy in June 1944.

They may have been technicians, but for the next year he and the observation post parties were frequently right at the sharp end, carrying out their vital role of pin-pointing German artillery and anti-aircraft batteries prior to their destruction by the British guns. When you hear all he has experienced, you will see why I find the word 'ordinary' a little inadequate in describing a man like Norman Cole. I am proud to have met him and I commend his book to you all.

Peter Hart
Oral Historian
Imperial War Museum

▲ Member of "A" Troop, 9th Survey Regiment on a short break for a swim near 'S-Hertogen-Bosch. I am top right in the picture.

The 1st Corp "Spearhead" shoulder badge.
The Surveyors 1st Class badge.
The Four Year's Service chevrons.
The Bombardier's stripes

Norman James Cole
in World War II

I was employed by Thos. Vanstone & Sons, Building Contractors as a Junior Surveyor. One or two days before war was declared, our firm was commissioned to visit several of the larger hotels in Torquay and to measure all the windows so that blackout screens could be manufactured and fitted, it being an offence to allow a light to be seen from inside the buildings. These hotels were soon taken over by the Royal Air Force to house men (and women?) to be trained as air-crew, etc.

Vanstones in conjunction with another contractor, were awarded a joint contract to 'splinter-proof' oil fuel tanks at Thankes, Torpoint, Plymouth. These tanks contained fuel oil for the Navy and, therefore, were of strategic importance for that Service. The work was considered to be of such importance that it was given "War Cabinet Priority", one of only two projects to be accorded this high level of priority. It meant in practice, that no matter what shortage there was for men or materials, our needs were met without delay. I remember a group of Irish labourers arriving on site to meet our requirements. The next day they did not turn up for work, but they were traced and made to return to the site. It was the same with materials. If we said that we needed 20 tons of cement in two days - despite the great shortages, 20 tons would arrive on time.

I remember a drunk Irishman arriving at the wooden site office, so drunk in fact that he could not get up the step to the door. He was told that if he came back the next day, sober, he could start work. He became the very best worker we had on site. The other bricklayers were forced to work harder to keep up with his work output.

The work comprised the building of a brickwork skin spaced out, I think about fifteen inches and then this space was filled in with concrete. The idea being that the splinters from bombs dropped nearby would not be able to puncture the tank sides and allow the fuel to escape.

The intense bombing of Plymouth took place whilst we were working there and a few of the tanks received direct hits and were set on fire.

I used to be driven to Thankes by the Manager in his small Opel car. On the morning following the Plymouth Blitz we were driving from Paignton towards Plymouth and, at some point beyond Ivybridge, we were stopped by a Military Despatch Rider. He had been told the car we would be travelling in and had been sent to intercept us and act as guide to get us to the site. The roads in Plymouth, due to the bombing, were mostly impassable. He took us on quite a circuitous route, eventually arriving at Plymouth Dockyard. We were given immediate entry and went to the river's edge and put onto an Admiral's Barge to get us across to the Thankes Depot on the other side of the river, such was the urgency given to the work we were undertaking.

The firemen were rushing to lay out their hoses to try to get control of the fires. Some of us volunteered to assist with carrying and rolling out the hoses. There was a considerable amount of thick black smoke and when I got home at the end of that day I remember my Mother saying "I didn't know whether to laugh or cry" because my face was black - as were my clothes. Within a day Ministry men arrived on our site with authority to make payment for any damage to our clothes. As you can imagine, even the labourers were also claiming for lost tools, etc. !!

The day following the night Blitz, some military personnel came and held a meeting in our site office. The purpose of their meeting was to decide what precautions could be taken to try and prevent the German airforce being able to send in reconnaissance planes to monitor the damage and to plan a further attack. I remember they were deciding where to locate defence barrage balloons.

There was a further incident on our site. One day a couple of our workmen brought in a man that they had discovered interfering with the fuel control valves. The man was, or pretended to be, deaf with no speech and no way of explaining his activities. We held him until we were able to get naval men to collect him and take him away. We never knew the outcome.

Before I finished at the site, there was one final incident. A naval rating brought to the office a colleague who had had an accident, causing a deep gash in his arm and obviously cutting through an artery. I was the person to administer First Aid on the site, so I put a dressing on the wound and applied a tourniquet to stop the flow of blood. I rushed him to the nearby doctor, who said that I should get him on the ferry back to Plymouth and to the hospital, in the meantime released the torniquet at intervals. We were able to get him to the hospital in time for treatment.

One other thing that I considered to be quite amazing. The day BEFORE the Plymouth Blitz, as we were travelling on the main road to Plymouth , there was a stationary queue of fire-engines from different parts of the country. Clearly intelligence had been received that the raid was going to take place. Full marks to our Code Breakers I suppose.

For two or three years prior to the outbreak of war I had a regular girl friend called Gwen. Gwen was a widow. She had been married, I am almost certain, in Hele Baptist Church, Torquay. Her husband, who was in the forces, was immediately sent to France and was killed, so that marriage had only lasted for two or three days. Shortly after war was declared, we decided to catch a bus to St. Marychurch and to walk along to Babbacombe, across Walls Hill, a headland jutting out towards the sea, and then back along the roads to Gwen's home. As we were walking across Walls Hill there was a sudden command "Halt! Who goes there?" We made a quick response, "Friends". It was a member of the Home Guard on patrol and he arrested us. We had no idea that there would be any military interest or activity in that area. I think we convinced him that we were not enemies, but he said that he had to escort us to his guardroom. We were duly questioned by the officer in charge, in quite a relaxed way and were soon 'released' and continued our journey back to Hele where Gwen lived with her mother.

Gwen had an unusually long stride pattern as she walked and, to tease me, Mary, my wife, used to refer to her as "Loopy Lou".

Another girl friend! There were German air attacks on Plymouth over a period prior to the major blitz on that city. As my home was on a road at the highest point above Paignton, it was possible to see what looked like a distant firework display as the bombs were dropping and the anti-aircraft guns were firing. The enemy planes flew, it seemed, right overhead as they made their way to Plymouth. For several evenings I went out on to the road to get the 'best' viewpoint as did a Mr. Fish and Joyce. It became a regular meeting for the three of us.

Joyce and I became very friendly, but it was a friendship which was constrained by the fact that Joyce was already engaged to an army serviceman. Joyce and I met at the week-ends and also in the evenings although it was dark, sitting in shelters, just enjoying each other's company and talking (in addition to eating chocolates!) Quite romantic, I suppose, in some ways, but we both knew that there was no long term future in the relationship.

CALL-UP

Eventually I received a notification telling me to report on a named date to the Exeter Castle for medical and general assessment, prior to my being called to the Military Services.

I duly reported and passed the medical examination. I was then questioned on a whole host of matters, qualifications, interests, etc. Part of the interview was to see if I had any preference as to which arm of the forces I would like to serve in. Prior to my interviews, there had been reports of a raid by Swordfish planes on two German battleships the Scharnhorst and the Gneiseneau. This had fired my imagination so I said I would like to serve in the Fleet Air Arm. They said it was not possible to go straight into the Fleet Air Arm, but that I should express a preference for the Royal Air Force with a second preference for the Navy. This I did and landed up in the Army - but this did really make sense and I will explain why.

When my call-up was received in February 1942, I was instructed to use the travel warrant which was enclosed and to travel to Wilton where there would be transport to take me to the Royal Artillery School of Survey at Larkhill on Salisbury Plain. On arrival there were the necessary registrations, being kitted out with soldier's uniform and other military accessories, including my first rifle. We were allocated our bed, locker , etc. in a large wooden hut. I think we then had our first taste of army food, and I always found it to be very good.

Within the first few days there were several medical parades for assessment, injections, etc. Two of the tests we had were 'General knowledge' and 'Mechanical knowledge'. In the former I came near the top, third I believe, but in the latter I came top. Most of the mechanical questions concerned situations with which I was familiar, having met the problems whilst using my favourite toy, Meccano. One problem - 'If on a bridge a railway engine was nearer to one end of the bridge, which abutment was bearing the greater load, or were they equally loaded? Another question was in the form of a diagram showing a series of pulleys, with a line over some and under others. The first pulley was rotating, say, in a clockwise direction, and the question was in which direction was the final pulley rotating?

At the same time we were split into two main divisions. These were "Sound Rangers" and "Flash Spotting" Units. I was allocated to the second of these.

Sound ranging was a system whereby using the time taken for the sound of a enemy gun firing to reach a series of microphones, the actual position of that gun could be located. I received no training in that sphere of activity so am unable to explain in any detail.

A Flash Spotter's primary role was to locate gun positions by plotting the direction of a gun flash from each of normally two or four posts in surveyed locations. These lines of sight were plotted in the Headquarters Unit, and from these plots the location of that firing gun was pin-pointed. In practice there were many more tasks undertaken, including plotting the spot where our planes were dropping their bombs to inform the RAF of their accuracy. There was also the general searching for targets by observing enemy positions, the activities of their tanks, etc. In effect we were the eyes of the Corps Headquarters and their heavy artillery units.

The training included the use and maintenance of surveying instruments, the most important one being what can best be described as a binocular theodolite. There was also instruction in the use of binoculars, range finders, magnetic compasses, and plane tables, the latter being used to plot map references, lines of sight, etc. as an alternative way of finding map locations. We were also instructed in advanced trigonometry, including moon, sun and star movements and the spherical trigonometry required in order to interpret the observations. We would not be handling them, but we had to learn about artillery guns and how they operated. We also learnt basic communication procedures using radio and morse code by telephone land lines.

Many of the calculations were performed using mechanical calculating machines (I purchased one from a shop in Hemel Hempstead after the war, and I still have it).

From each posting in this country we received instruction in driving various types of vehicles including cars, trucks small and large, motor cycles, etc. This was to form part of the skills I had to acquire in order to be awarded my Surveyors Proficiency First Class Badge, a "S" inside a laurel wreath. Winning the Surveyor's badge meant an increase in pay.

A few happenings outside of the actual training. Firstly there was an incident which arose from our training. There was at the School of Survey a line of marked spots on the ground, the map references of each being accurately known. We had to set up our instruments over one of these positions and then by measuring lines of sight to known objects such as church towers, windpumps, etc. we were able to assess the map reference of that particular point. One of the Instructors had a favourite man and to help him to pass the test, he actually gave him a list of the map references of each of the locations. The only problem was that he gave him the references for a completely different location. So when that soldier submitted his observation results what had happened became very clear. I assume that the man failed and that the Instructor was dismissed.

One day there was a request for anyone who could use a builder's dumpy level to report to the office. I was the only person who had knowledge of site levelling using that instrument so volunteered. I was given a small estate car and two soldiers and given the freedom to go anywhere on Salisbury Plain and try to find a location one hundred yards square where the ground level did not vary by more than twelve inches. We could go on any land, whether private or otherwise, but after what I think was a couple of days, failed to find anywhere that met the criteria. Some locations looked completely flat but on measuring the levels over the whole area, found levels differing by more than the permitted amount. I don't think we were told the object of the exercise, but believed that it was something to do with laying out a mesh aerial on the ground as part of the development of radar.

One day we were in the gymnasium for exercises, when we were given boxing gloves and asked to spar with someone. The Physical Instructors were watching us and afterwards five or six of us had to stay behind. We were told that we were to form part of the School's boxing team and would get special training (and also some extra food!). Eventually we were to compete against a Field Gun Regiment stationed nearby. On the day of the contest, I remember sitting in the dressing room and also in the room was another soldier, all kitted up and ready for the ring. I asked him his name and he turned out to be my opponent. I saw his broken nose and asked him if he had done much boxing before this. He said that he had done some. I wondered what I was in for. In fact it was a very close contest and I lost on points, but was completely unmarked.

Another sporting moment. Our Colonel wanted to raise a basketball team, a game I suppose we played in the gym from time to time. I was selected to be one of the team. I can't remember anything of the game or games we played but I do remember that the Colonel gave each of us ten shillings for being in his team. I was, therefore, actually paid for playing basketball. I have as a result often jokingly stated that I was at one time a professional basketball player!

One other memory of Larkhill was that the ATS girls who served us our food commented that when I laughed, my eyes were clearly laughing. As a result I was nicknamed by them, "Laughing Eyes".

After three or six month's training, I can't remember which, we were posted from the School of Survey to an operating Regiment. My posting was to the 9th Survey Regiment R.A. stationed at Coxhoe, a village to the South of Durham. Whilst we were stationed there we were taken to a school and introduced to a Lieutenant Kubista, a Czech who was to instruct us in "Silent Killing". The object of this training was that as we would be operating at or very near to the front line, there would be the possibility that a stray German might discover our camouflaged observation post. It would then be necessary to ensure he could not disclose our position to his forces. We learnt how to kill a German using his own battle-dress, how to render him unable to shout without killing him, how to hold him immobile with just one hand, how to fix him to a post so that he could not escape or even in such a position that he could not escape and in the eventuality that we were unable to return to take him prisoner, he would die in less than half an hour. Nothing else notable or exciting that I can remember about that location and after a time we were moved to Carlbury near Piercebridge. Again it was routine training and practice. The one unusual job was to take a vehicle to the nearby river, collect stones, bring them back to the field where our huts were located and use them to build a road into the site from the approach lane.

The first day there, I was on an informal guard duty at the entrance and two sisters walked down the land and stopped to talk. They invited me to visit them at home. Their father was the railway crossing keeper and the family had me down there a couple of times for tea, so I was given the temporary nick-name of 'Cole, the crossing sweeper'.

I was instructed to take a vehicle and its driver to Catterick, Yorkshire, to collect a motor bike. We duly arrived at the depot and I was taken to the point where the bike was ready for collection. I suppose I must have signed the necessary document and the soldier handed the bike to me. That is where it went wrong. I had no idea how heavy the machine would be and, as he handed it over, it started to overbalance away from me and I couldn't stop it crashing to the ground. The outcome, one bike with a control lever broken off. I think I might hold the record for having in possession a motor bike the shortest amount of time before crashing it !!

We did a couple of training exercises that stuck in my memory. A Nissen hut which was full of military supplies and equipment had been booby-trapped. Trip wires and book-flap devices had been wired up to detonators which would explode if disturbed. I had to take a small team from one end of the hut to exit at the other end, disarming the booby-traps as we went without detonating any of the traps. At one point I carefully lifted a coil of camouflage tape to feel if there was a book-flap underneath. Just as I did so a nearby detonator exploded! Me, the leader of the team, had failed to discover a booby-trap - but no I hadn't, it was someone else who had caused the explosion, but at exactly the same moment as I had lifted the camouflage bale. I was much relieved when I discovered that I wasn't guilty.

Another exercise involved entering a wood and getting through it without setting off any booby-traps. There were also cut-outs representing enemy troops hidden among the trees, which we had to discover and shoot at. The path I was following came to a "T" junction and I had to go to the left. It struck me that as I turned to go left, my back would be exposed to an enemy soldier hidden somewhere away to my right. There was one, partially hidden in a tree. Apparently I was one of the very few who had thought of protecting the rear on turning the corner, and was commended for that.

Our next posting was to Alyth in Scotland, not far from Dundee. That move was as a result of our being transferred to 1st Corps which had been selected to be the spearhead of the coming attack on northern France. This was in keeping with our shoulder badges, which had a white spearhead on a diamond shaped badge coloured blue and red, the colours of the Royal Artillery.

From that posting we were to do a lot of Commando mountain warfare training. Besides exercising our own skills, we went to different Regiments to demonstrate to them what we were able to do and to explain how they would use us in actual combat.

We also did some gun calibration. This was to check the accuracy of each gun's sighting equipment. This was done by each gun firing a round, sometimes out to sea, and we would plot the spot where the shell actually landed. They then could compare the actual position with the information they had fed into their gunsights, thereby checking its accuracy, and this enabled them to make any necessary corrections.

We didn't know it at the time, but the officers of our unit were, under great secrecy, taken to the River Clyde where there were LST's (Landing Ship Tank) awaiting them. They had to familiarise themselves with driving vehicles up the ramp to get aboard the craft and later to drive them down the ramp into water some two to three feet deep. They also had to practice the skill of clambering down nets to access the LSTs. Situations we were going to meet during the invasion!

The mountain training had many aspects. There was the obvious getting us used to climbing mountains carrying our heavy equipment and then setting up observation posts on the tops of the mountains. We did some of this training in the vicinity of Loch Tay. Just north of the Loch is Ben Lawers, a mountain 1214 feet high. We had to climb this one from side to side.

The purpose of one of these mountain exercises was to test our efficiency in camouflaging our positions. We had to climb a mountain (I thought it was called Carn Na Brochaid, but I can't find it on any map so perhaps that is incorrect) with all of our equipment, laying out a telephone cable as we progressed, so that we could communicate with ground level. Across the valley on the facing mountain, there was a group of officers with binoculars attempting to locate our observation post set-up. This went well until it was time to pack up and reel in the telephone wire. After a while we were unable to keep the wire coming in, it seemed to be caught on something. We had to climb back to locate the problem and found that a sheep had stepped into a loop in the wire and it was wound around its leg. We had been unknowingly pulling the sheep down the mountain side!

Our camouflage was effective because we were not spotted by the observers. The road alongside Loch Tay was the location for another toughening up exercise. We had to carry our full pack and rifles and run the length of the Loch, about 12 miles, within a set time, which meant that we had to run for most of the time. Then as we neared the end, we had to pick up a colleague with all his equipment and run for 200 yards in, I think 90 seconds, and then exchange places and run the 200 yards back in the same time.

Whilst stationed at Alyth, General Montgomery issued an order that everyone who undertook mountain Commando training was to be given a one week's break. This didn't mean home holiday but just enjoying sports, competitions, etc.

We had one officer who was very much disliked. 'Gumrot', for that was the name we gave him, relished a sense of power over 'other ranks' and could be quite vindictive. Ability we respected but this form of bullying was not acceptable.

For some reason which I cannot remember, I had to go to the house where the officers were billeted and I was in the kitchen where a meal was being prepared. I was probably scrounging a cup of tea! One of the cooks said to me "This ham sandwich is for Gumrot". He then placed on the worktop a piece of bread, and on it the slices of ham. He then spat on it and put on the upper piece of bread - all ready to be served up to Gumrot.

On one of the regular morning parades, Gumrot was the inspecting officer. When he came to inspect my rifle he said that there was rust in the barrel; there wasn't, but he awarded me three days extra guard duty as a punishment. After the parade I went to the RSM (Regimental Sergeant Major), explained what had happened and invited him to inspect my rifle. He didn't need to because he accepted what I had said to him. His advice was "Just do the guard duty, it will be easier than trying to get him to change his decision". He knew what Gumrot was like.

I understood that our Sergeant Major went to the Captain and said that he could not be responsible for that officer's safety in battle situations i.e. someone might do him some harm. The Captain must have had a talk with him and he completely changed. One of the competitions that was arranged during this break period was for four teams, each to have a cable laying hand truck, lay a cable across the River Tay which was adjacent to where we spent this particular week, and get a phone connected to the other side. 'Gumrot' asked if he could be in one of the teams and actually took part with other ranks in that competition. Officers and other ranks would not normally mix in such things. Also in that week, there was an impromptu entertainment show and 'Gumrot' did one of the turns, and actually referred to himself as Gumrot.

An important VIP, a General, was due to travel up through Scotland by road. We were instructed to act as traffic controllers to ensure that there were no delays to his progress. A few of us were sent with our 15 cwt truck to the centre of Balmoral, the town with many royal connections. We were on location a long time before the General was due to pass our way, so we decided there was time for a meal. I undertook the preparation of the potatoes. Has anyone else ever sat on a seat in the sedate centre of Balmoral peeling potatoes? I guess not!

A girl from Dundee came to visit her friend in Alyth. Somehow I came in contact with them and both of them invited me to visit them in their respective homes. It meant that during the week I could visit the home in Alyth. Imagine my horror on finding that our Regimental Sergeant Major had also been invited there by an older sister. I was very careful to avoid any suggestion, both in the home and also when on parade, that there had been this contact.

The Dundee girl, Chrissie, became a very close friend. She was a very talented violinist and was a teacher of that instrument at the Dundee Academy of Music. She had even been invited to go on tour with the then famous Ivy Benson and her All Ladies Band - but, as she had a widowed mother decided not to accept the offer. She was involved with a little concert party called "The Blackout Scandals". Besides Chrissie on the violin, there was her sister, Jean, on the piano accordion and the Spanish Consul's daughter, Biddy, on the piano. There was also a man singer/comedian and a dance team of three or four girls. This concert party used to visit local village halls, army camps, etc. Whenever I could, I went with them and helped to carry equipment.

One incident so intrigued me that I have never forgotten it. We were in the local Co-op hall for a practice session. Nicky (L.R.A.M.!) was in the body of the hall taking the dancers through some Irish dance routine. The band was on the platform where the piano was located. Nicky told the band to practice their musical items and, as they did so, Nicky suddenly shouted to them "Go back three bars" and then again, "There is somebody playing a wrong note". It was Biddy on the piano playing one incorrect note and although Nicky was concentrating on the dancers, she had picked up that small mistake.

In the second week of November 1943 our time at Alyth came to an end and we moved down south to Johnstone, a suburb of Glasgow but this stop was only for a few days and then we were on the move, again southwards and into an army camp in Cobham, Surrey. We were in huts in the grounds of a large house and our daily activities were in the nature of maintaining our fitness and refreshing our memories on all that we had been taught. It was obvious that we were becoming part of a major concentration of troops in the south of England in preparation for an invasion of the continent.

It was also clear that we would be landing in shallow water off a beach as we had to learn how to waterproof vehicles and equipment. Our transport might not be able to get close enough to enable us to land on dry land.

On Christmas Day I walked to a church which had a canteen available to the forces. They had arranged for us to watch a film, "Mrs. Miniver", and I remember thinking how commendable it was that those ladies had given up being home on Christmas Day to entertain us. As I was walking back towards camp I was passing houses with celebrations probably going on inside. I was longing for someone inside to hear the clanking of my boots on the pavement and invite me in to join them - but nobody did.

Another time I went to that same church canteen and got caught in a London pea-souper fog. It is difficult to describe this if you haven't been in one. It is impossible to see beyond one or two metres ahead. I tried to follow the house boundaries as I walked along the path. After a while I realised I was walking on gravel and not the hard paving. I edged slowly ahead keeping on the gravel, and came to a large house. I found a window with a railing guard outside and felt my way along this until I came to a door. I rang the bell and a man came out and took me back down their drive until I was on the road again. Just at that moment an AA man on a motor bike and sidecar came very slowly into view. He had altered his headlight so that it was shining down on to the white line in the middle of the road. I followed him up the road to the T junction which was very near to the camp entrance, and found my way to my hut.

Whilst stationed at Cobham, there was posted on our notice board a request for anyone wishing to be considered for training as an Officer to sign their name on the sheet. I was not interested in leaving my unit to go to OCTU (Officer Cadet Training Unit), the reason being that I was doing a technical role which had similarities to my civilian profession as a surveyor. I really did enjoy the surveying and target spotting work and had no wish at all to go as an officer in what would probably be a non-technical unit. I didn't sign.

Our Captain ordered a colleague and myself to meet him in his office. He tried to get us to change our minds by saying that the Brigadier or someone was keen to get our acceptance of the offer. The notice was removed and a new notice took its place and this time my colleague, Sgt. Wick's name and my name was already printed on the notice, so we both deleted our names and didn't hear anything more.

Many years after the war the B.B.C. invited ex-servicemen to send in details of their military experiences. One who did so was Ron Bromley who, whilst a gunner, had also been recommended for officer training. He accepted this and was posted to 121 OCTU at Aldershot. After passing out he was posted to the 9th Survey Regiment, my regiment! So now I am left wondering if, by accepting the offer of officer training, instead of landing in a non-technical regiment as I had presumed, I might have returned to a survey regiment after all.

I was granted a short home leave and it was great to have some time with my parents.

One day, in uniform, I went down to Paignton town centre to do some shopping. Whilst I was inside Woolworths, a little child came running up to me shouting, much to his mother's embarrassment, "Daddy, Daddy". Presumably his father was also in the forces, hence his mistake.

That same day, I had a cough and felt a bit 'chesty'. Our leave details stated that if we needed any medical attention or medication whilst on leave, we were to report to the nearest hospital. So on my way home I called in at Paignton Hospital and asked if they could let me have some cough medicine. A Nursing Sister came and took my temperature and said "I can't just give you medicine. You have a high temperature so I have to admit you as a patient." This was a problem because my parents would have expected me to return home from the shopping trip and here I was being kept in hospital. In those days my parents did not have a telephone and would have been worried at my non-appearance. I asked the nurse to contact my previous employers, Thos. Vanstone & Sons in Torquay and asked if their Manager who lived in Paignton could call on my parents and explain what had happened. He did just that. They came to visit me and to collect the shopping.

I was kept in hospital for a few days and built up a rapport with some of the nurses. One in particular kept teasing me, so on the day I was due to be released, whilst she was teasing me, I picked her up, carried her into the bathroom, and dumped her in the bath. (No I didn't turn the taps on!) Notwithstanding that, I invited her to come up to my home at the top of Paignton, meet my parents and have tea with us. I did meet her and brought her home for tea but I never saw her again after that.

I left Cobham one fine Summer's day and headed straight into the centre of London and down to the dock areas of Canning Town which had suffered badly from the Blitz days. Barbed wire enclosed camps had been built on the demolished house sites and in one of these we were accommodated. We were for security reasons, confined to camp and the only time we could get out was to get to our car park about half a mile distant, and then only in organised marching parties. In this area the dockers lived and believe me, they were generous in the extreme to troops. On our journey in we had to go in slow easy stages when near the embarcation area owing to the great number of convoys on the move, and all the time there were jugs of tea, cakes, lemonade, cigarettes, etc. in plenty. It was obvious that everyone knew what was afoot - the person would be stupid that didn't realise.

As soon as we were installed in this camp, someone outside rigged up a loudspeaker from their wireless set to entertain us and let us hear the news bulletins. I won't go into details of what we did, most of it was painting ship numbers etc. on to the trucks which wouldn't be very interesting to you. In these camps, incidentally, were large NAAFIs staffed by girl volunteers. They too for security reasons were unable to get outside the barbed wire.

All our moving orders and instructions for drawing 24 hour rations, Mae Wests, vomit bags (Yes! In case of seasickness in the ships' holds) etc., were given over mobile loudspeakers.

Operation Overlord

One of the first things organised was to issue us with emergency rations and to give a demonstration on how to use them. There was a very simple solid fuel burner and fuel tablets, tablets that when water was added and then heated became soup. Other tablets could be made into tea complete with milk, hard biscuits, chocolate bars, etc. all in one small package. The demonstrator "borrowed" my pack and used it for his demonstration, which meant that I was left without one. I had a dickens of a job to get a replacement.

We were only there for a couple of days before we had orders to get loaded with all our equipment, so complete that it was known as full battle order. We then marched out of the barbed wire enclosed camp and were loaded on to London Transport double-decker busses. We barely had time to get settled when we were given the order to de-bus and we were marched back to the camp site. We now know that this was due to D-Day being postponed for twenty four hours. The next day we were again loaded on to the buses and driven to the Royal Docks on the River Thames. We boarded a large freight type ship and as I looked down on to the dockside, there was an elderly lady waving and crying. She was clearly disturbed at the thought of what we were about to do.

On board we slept on palliasses or else in hammocks, down in the holds, some even slept on deck.

The boat we were on was one of a class made in America and all had a name starting with the word "Empire". Ours was the "Empire Deeds".

As we went down the river we passed the Ford Motor Works and there were a lot of the workers on the roof where they had a loudhailer. They sent a message to us "Empire Deeds Ahoy, Empire Deeds Ahoy, good luck and good hunting".

A little later there was a point where railway lines were adjacent to the river. On them were some locomotives and as we sailed past them they started sounding their whistles in greeting, and some of them were doing the 'dot, dot, dot, dash' "V" for victory sign.

One thing that I thought was rather naughty, was that of all the vehicles which were already loaded, the ambulances were on the upper deck - so from the air it might give the impression that ours was a hospital ship. We were told to take our mess tins to the galley to get some food. This consisted of some soup with half a tin of salmon in one tin and tea in the other. All meals from this central cookhouse were very good.

Whilst on the boat I met a fellow who used to be with me in the Boys' Brigade, quite a co-incidence, eh?

On the journey we were told that we were approaching the Straits of Dover and convoys were sometimes shelled. We were given 'abandon ship' orders, fire orders, etc. by the Captain speaking through a loudspeaker. Gosh! We started to shiver in our shoes. Luckily for us a mist developed and we got through unscathed.

After a couple of days we awoke one morning to see that we were steaming for land and for the most marvellous scene ever. Hundreds of ships of all sorts and sizes spread out as far as the eye could see. Warships steaming up and down the coast and occasionally a stationary cruiser shelling the shore. No words could ever describe the scene and I guess pictures in the papers will have given you a little idea.

The big ships were still and fussing around them were landing barges, speedboats, DUCKS, etc. all getting loads from the steamers and then disgorging them on to the beaches.

On the way over, I did go on deck and saw one boat stationary and burning, presumably having been attacked by a motor torpedo boat, or hit by a bomb.

An explanation of the term 'DUCKS'. These were load carrying vehicles that could travel on land or on water. Although they were always described as 'Ducks', the correct military name is 'DUKW'. The 'D'=designed in 1942, 'U' = utility (amphibious), 'K' all wheel drive and 'W'= two powered rear axles.

My next memory is of being stationary off the beach with HMS Warspite behind us firing shells on to the land. As you will have seen from the many books, films, etc. it was intense activity all along the shore and much noise from the guns firing and from shells landing on the beach from the German guns and mortars. Watching the explosions on the beach, I thought that the Royal

Engineers were there clearing the beach of mines, and I did not realise that it was shells and mortars exploding.

We were told to get completely kitted up and ready to disembark. With the weight of our packs, rifle, etc. it was not easy to scramble down to a tank landing craft which had drawn up alongside. This craft drove us in to the beach and, as the tide was going out, were soon able to step off without stepping into water. I wrote home and said that "whilst waiting there we could look out to sea and see the terrific armada of ships of all sorts and sizes." It was then a case of getting up the beach to where the Beach Control Officer was dug into the bank and to hand to him one of the slips named for this purpose. These perforated slips were part of a long strip, each slip printed to indicate its use, the first one was handed in when we left the barbed wire enclosed camp, the next when we boarded the boat at the Royal Docks, then as we left the boat and then this final one to be handed to the Beach Control Officer. This latter one, obviously, to register the fact that we had landed safely. A copy of the unused portion of similar slips headed '112 Transit Camp, Camp No.3' (Plate 1).

Running up the beach we kept away from areas marked "Achtung Minen", (Beware Mines). The beach we had landed on was part of "Sword" beach and was at the village of Lion-sur-Mere.

After crossing the lane we were directed into a large slightly sloping field where areas had been marked out in squares with white tape. We were to go into one of these squares which was for Artillery personnel. The officers went to receive instructions from the beach organisers and we snatched a short rest. We hadn't come far but we were in Assault Landing Order (carrying everything we owned) so we were tired. This was only the start and we had to march on for another mile or so before we reached our resting place for the night. It was here that we had our first meal from the 24 hour ration packs. Each of these packs, incidentally, being small enough to fit in a mess tin and yet made three good meals each day. The first person we saw was a French civilian with a bicycle, standing watching us. We also saw a man walking along with a little girl. The girl was jabbering away in French and I thought , "What a clever girl she can speak French" - then the penny dropped and I thought, you fool, of course she can speak French we're in France. From then to the time we reached our resting place, we were all the time passing between 'Achtung Minen' signs which Jerry hadn't had time to remove. The first village we hit was Gray-sur-Mer about 300 yards from the beaches.

Although we didn't know it at the time, the German 21st Panzer Division attempted to drive to the coast and isolate Sword Beach from the rest of the invasion landings. They didn't succeed, but I have since read that the Allied

◀ Plate 1

Part of the strip of tickets that had to be handed in at stages from embarkation to landing.

▼ Plate 2

Envelope for use by soldiers on active service when sending a letter containing nothing but private and family affairs.

Command were quite prepared for the Eastern end of the beachhead to be cut off and lost to the enemy. That was us! They saw that it would even then, have a purpose in causing a diversion from the main drive to Caen.

We started to dig in, when the guard we had set up reported that there was movement in a nearby wood. Snipers had been there only a few hours earlier so we soon got ourselves into a kind of investigating patrol, well armed, and carefully crept towards the edge of the wood, but then we discovered that the sounds had been made by one of the few cows that remained alive.

Sgt. Wicks took a Jeep and went down the road which we had reached, and he didn't return for what must have been some hours. He was fluent in the German language. He didn't realise that he had strayed into territory still in German hands, and of course was taken prisoner. If I remember rightly, he was taken to a cave occupied by German troops. The battle front was very fluid and uncertain at that time; in other words there wasn't a clear front line of demarcation between the two armies. Apparently Sgt. Wicks convinced the Germans that they were surrounded and that they had better surrender. They believed him (and in the circumstances it might have been true) and they allowed him to bring them back as prisoners themselves.

From that place we were sent to a typical French hedgerow, I believe somewhere near Aubin de Arquinay (?spelling?) There were two lines of thick hedge with a space like a footpath between them. When we got to this site, we found that there were infantry soldiers dug into trenches facing in both directions. This was like a finger running up into German territory, so there were Germans on both sides of us. We had to dig our trenches for protection and then set up our observation equipment, ready to look for targets for our artillery.

Whilst we were there a sergeant was killed and buried by his mates alongside where there were eight other new graves. It was here that I learnt the art of diving into a trench as soon as we heard 'Wheeow, wheeow, wheeow' of Moaning Minnies or Sobbing Sisters, our nicknames for German rocket mortars. We were able to get water from a pump in a farmyard behind us. Once we had a couple of our fellows there when the spot was shelled and we spent an anxious few minutes looking for the first glimpse of them. They were o.k. These latter details were taken from a letter sent home in an "Active Service Army Privilege Envelope"(Plate 2)

After a while an Officer came along and asked if anyone had black plimsolls that he could 'borrow'. With him were two soldiers in camouflage uniform with their faces all blackened. They were, in the night, to make contact with the local French underground unit, the Maquis. The soldiers were very relieved to learn that that contact had had to be abandoned, and that they could stand down. During the previous night some mines had been laid outside the hedges to give us added protection.

During the very short time that we were in that hedge, nothing of note happened, no enemy fire landed near to us.

A RAMC (Royal Army Medical Corps) sergeant came alongside us and started a conversation. He told us that he had been in Dunkirk. He said "I was down in my hole once and the stuff was dropping all ways. Suddenly I heard one that seemed to be coming straight for me. I turned around and I saw a worm coming through the end, so I pulled him out and got right in its hole." A touch of humour in a dangerous situation.

As you can imagine, the days immediately following the landings, were occupied in battle conditions, which meant staying alive and being at all times ready to defend oneself. It was the 12th June 1944 before I was able to write my first letter to home. As I was writing, I didn't know what I should give as my address for reply. When I had finished, I made enquiries and discovered that there had been no time to change from my last address in England - A Troop, B Battery, 9th Survey Regiment R.A., A.P.O., England. So there I was in France with an English address!

In my next letter to home I wrote

"I myself am now quite an expert at digging deep trenches in a very short time and also at taking headers into them without hurting myself. I was laid here in a trench and could hear someone reading aloud from a newspaper on our life out here. It said that the boys had left their holes in the ground for the nearest barn. Grrr ! Words failed me. Just a few yards along from my trench there were nine little wooden crosses over the graves of some of the unlucky ones".

A sergeant was recently buried there and I noticed that some of his pals had scrounged some roses and placed them at the foot.

Very soon we were in an area where there was and had been a great amount of fighting. We came across many dead Germans and left them to be dealt with by the appropriate workers. We also found a dead English soldier that no-one had had the time to bury. We hurriedly began digging a grave for him. I took the documents from his uniform as these could be passed down to Headquarters for record purposes. As we were burying him my signaller, not a Christian by any means asked if it was possible to hold a short committal 'service', and he wanted to do it. I was the only one with a Bible, which he borrowed and then asked me what he could read. I suggested the obvious text that came to mind, the 23rd Psalm. He read this Scripture and we duly buried the man.

Several days later we had to retrace our steps along this road for some purpose, and we saw that where we had buried the man, actually in someone's garden, the grave had been provided with a surround consisting of white painted wood and I'm sure there were flowers there.

Whilst in a dugout which had to be well camouflaged, I was observing the enemy troops and their tanks in and around the edge of some woodland. They were completely unaware that they could be seen from our side of the front line. I suddenly noticed one of their soldiers come out to the front of the woods and give himself a strip wash. He presumably was embarrassed to wash himself in front of his comrades. Little did he know that I was watching his every move and could easily have shot him. If I had done so it would have given away my hidden position. It wasn't very long before I saw our tanks approaching the enemy positions and a tank battle ensued. I can't remember, but no doubt I was informing our operations control centre of what was happening and monitoring the success, or otherwise, of the attack, that being my role in such circumstances.

We had instructions to move to another location and set up our observation post. As usual we would have been given the exact map reference and this was to locate a Maternity Home at Benouville, very near to the Caen Canal and to Pegasus Bridge. On the way we passed a group of the Parachute Corps, the men who had landed and captured the bridge over the canal. They were waiting to be picked up and flown back to Britain to be ready for operation in some other area of war.

Nearby were scattered the gliders which had brought the 6th Airlanding Brigade for their attack on the Pegasus Bridge. These were all over the place, some intact but some had been badly damaged on landing.

We were moving forward in convoy when we were shelled by the enemy. The driver of one truck was so frightened that, when the road bore around to the left, he didn't turn, but drove straight ahead and into a field. His pal, Gnr. Savage, hauled him out of the driver's seat saying, in what I expect were no uncertain terms, "Get out, I'll drive". We got the vehicle back on to the road and the journey continued.

On arrival at the Maternity Home, the obvious place for the observation post was on the roof of the building. We got set up and then in the night shells started to fall almost on top of us. The scream of the shells was almost deafening, so needless to say we quickly made our way into the building and safety. It was jet black. I woke up the others who were still asleep and got them moving down out of the way. We went down a couple of flights of stairs and made for the centre of the building. We were groping around for an alcove that we knew existed, when suddenly a shell dropped right beside us and all the glass came in and we were sprayed with water. Of course we thought a main had been burst. In the morning we found our mistake, someone had accidentally knocked over a fire extinguisher. Did we laugh? When the period of shelling had stopped we went back to the equipment left on the roof. After a while the Matron of the Maternity Home said that it was not right for us to be on the building, as the roof had painted on it a red cross to inform aircraft that this was not a military target, but a hospital. As a result of her request, we moved from the Hospital roof and relocated in the top section of a water tower in the middle of a wood in the home's grounds. Realising that as we would be at the top of a winding staircase, the enemy could come to the bottom of the tower and throw in a hand grenade, we needed to have warning. So we put a tripwire across the entrance leading to some empty tins so that catching the wire would cause the tins to make a din, and we would know that there was someone below. We had our own hand grenades, which we could then have thrown down to eliminate the danger below us.

Pictures of the Maternity Home were published in a British Illustrated magazine (Pages 37-40). I know some of the people in the pictures. Therese the pharmacist who became a friend of mine is seen on Page 40, the bottom left hand photo (interior of a church); Therese is second from the right.

In addition to the shelling from the usual artillery and mortars, the Germans had a very heavy gun at Merville, to the East of our location. We understood that this gun was in a special emplacement where it came to the surface to fire and then descended into an underground bunker. It was of a exceptionally large calibre and therefore fired an enormous shell. It was the only gun that I met, where the sound of its firing arrived before the actual shell. One day I was walking across the area in front of the Maternity Home when I heard this gun fire. There was then an enormous explosion. The shell had landed quite nearby. This was the only time that I panicked. I started to run and believe I just ran in a circle because I had no idea where to go. After a few moments I clearly calmed down and went about my business and fortunately there no further shells from that gun. Rightly or not I don't know, but we were told that that gun emplacement had been bombed and shelled, but the gun was still active so in the end, Commandos were sent in and physically spiked the gun. (Spiking is the act of causing an explosion actually in the barrel of the gun to destroy it).

SINCE D-DAY EIGHTEEN BABIES HAVE BEEN BROUGHT INTO THE WORLD IN CELLARS OF THIS MATERNITY HOME ON THE BANKS OF THE CAEN CANAL, EXPOSED TO ARTILLERY FIRE FOR MANY WEEKS

MATERNITY HOME WAS IN THE FRONT LINE

Matron, midwife and nurses carried on devotedly for weeks while all around them raged the battle for Caen. Newly-born babies enjoyed normal welfare treatment

THE front line in a long-continued battle is hardly a propitious site for a maternity home, yet no fewer than eighteen babies—all girls—were born at an institution on the banks of the Caen canal during a period of weeks while the struggle for the ancient Norman city was at the height of its ferocity.

This institution, the Benouville Maternity Home and Orphanage, happened to be on a spot near which, on D-Day, British paratroops landed and dug themselves in—an operation witnessed by the matron of the home, Madame Lea Vion a fifty-four years old Parisienne who served as a nurse during the last war.

Madame Vion and her midwife, Madame Lesfourges, with their nursing staff, have proved themselves worthy compatriots of Joan of Arc. Undeterred by almost continuous shellfire and all the horrors of battle, they carried on with their duties, giving mothers and babies the best of their skill.

Most of the work, of course, had to be done down in the cellar of the home, a damp place lighted only by acetylene lamps and by no means ideal for the function of accouchement. In the intervals of battle, patients fit to be moved were brought into the fresh air; the others, of course, had to remain where they were.

Close by the hospital is the thirteenth-century parish church of Blainville. Its resident priest, Abbé Saint-Jean, was frequently in demand for christening the newly-arrived citizens of the French Republic. He, like the hospital matron and her assistants, stuck to his post of duty throughout all the troublous period, until at last the tide of battle ebbed away far to the east and tranquillity and peace once again descended on Normandy.

OVER▶

Hospital Matron Madame Lea Vion saw British paratroops take the nearby Benouville bridge across the Caen Canal

Hospital Midwife is Madame Lesfourges, seen here with baby Raymond Mongoubert, a great favourite at the home

Anxious Period for expectant mothers, who, when enemy fire was hot, used to knit and sleep down in the cellar

Operating Theatre down in the cellar where, by the light of small acetylene lamps and under the most primitive conditions, eighteen babies have been ushered into this troubled world since the sixth of June last to the accompaniment outside of the ceaseless roar of artillery, punctuated by screaming shells and the sickening crump of high explosives

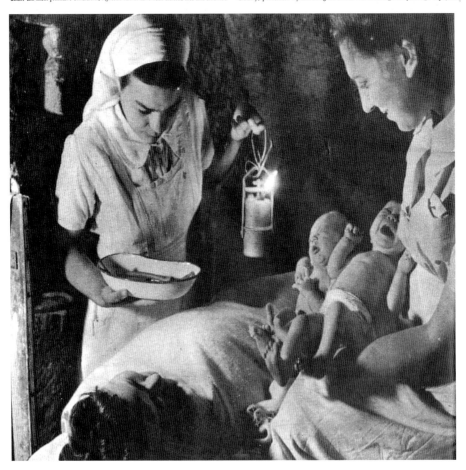

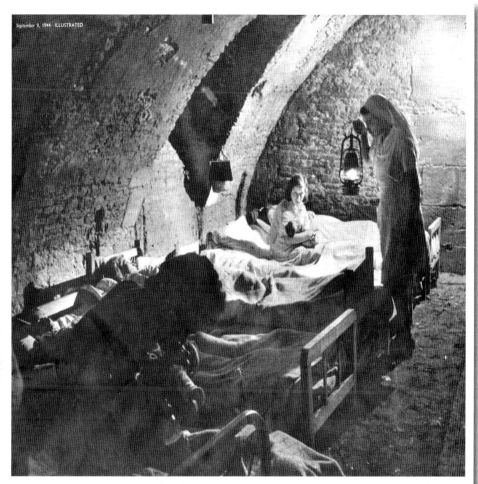

After Childbirth the mothers lie comfortably with their babies in another part of the dimly lighted cellar, where Madame Vion and Madame Lesfourges lavish on them the utmost care until they are able to get back to their homes—if they still have homes to go to. It is hard to imagine any less propitious circumstances for the start of a young life

Preparing Milk for the babies; Mme Vion looks on with one of the orphans—the hospital is also an orphanage

Washing Babies at the entrance to the cellar is one of those happy occasions when the mothers relish a gossip

The Newly Born, despite its inauspicious surroundings, enjoys all the attentions a skilled nurse can give it

Careful Records are kept for welfare purposes, and here you see Mme Vion recording the weight of a newly born

Lulls In Battle provide the opportunities such as this when the babies are taken from the cellar to fresh air

Baptismal Service for newly borns held in the chapel of Blainville by Abbé Saint-Jean, curé of the parish. All the time the ceremony was in progress, nearby artillery was firing and the windows of the chapel were rattling incessantly

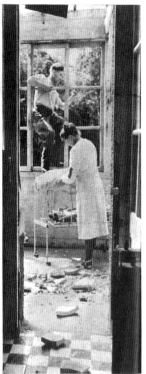

There's A War On, and from time to time for many weeks the hospital staff had to get help to clear away debris

Whenever it seemed that there was a lull in the shelling, the Hospital used to get the mothers in the Maternity Home to come out into the open air, because they were normally indoors and even sheltering in the cellars for protection. We cruelly referred to this as 'the parade of the pregs', but the attached photos show the terrible conditions in which they were living and getting medical assistance.

We soon made friends with the girls and a couple of men who were staff of the Home. Therese the Pharmacist and I became friends. Andree, one of the men, also became a friend there.

One day as I was walking across the open area in front of the hospital building, a soldier staggered out of the edge of the woods and collapsed. I understood from what he was able to tell me, that he had been with an armoured column and had been repeatedly shelled. After a period of persistent shelling, his nerve had gone and had run away from his unit and into the woods.

With a colleague I got the man on to a stretcher and took him into the hospital for help. The Pharmacist assessed the man's condition and gave him an injection.

I needed to record the soldier's condition and also the medical treatment he had received. This being in active war conditions, there was no time to get hold of paper to note the details. All I had was a letter which I had received from my Mother. I took out the actual letter and used the back of the envelope to make notes realising that this information would be needed by medical staff (Plate 4).

My colleague and I then carried the stretchered man back through the woods to the main road - solid with military vehicles slowly moving up to the front line. One of these vehicles was a canvas sided ambulance. When the driver saw us, he asked if we were trying to get the man to a medical station, and on answering in the affirmative, he said "Get him in the back and one of you come with him".

Fortunately, despite only having canvas sides to the vehicle, we were not hit. Already in the ambulance were wounded soldiers on stretchers, one of which was an army sergeant who had a large black "M" on his forehead to show that he had been given a morphine injection. He asked me to give him a cigarette. I found one and lit it for him, We got to an R.A.M.C. forward medical centre, a large tent over a depression in the ground, where there were medical attendants and presumably doctors. We left the shell-shocked victim in their care and they were delighted with the envelope notes as they knew where to start their assessment (Plate 4). They told me that, after treatment, the man would be taken back to the beachhead and transported back to England.

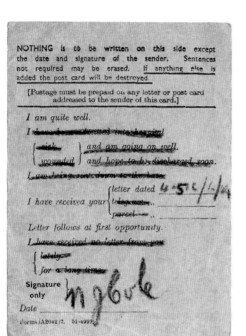

◀ Plate 3

First communication to home in the form of a Field Service Post Card

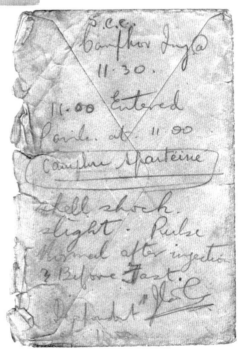

▶ Plate 4

Notes on condition and treatment of shell-shocked soldier

We had been working, locating targets in preparation for the assault on Caen. We had seen the results of our work in the terrific artillery barrage during that attack. This was so intense that I said at the time that I thought that France could be cracked in half.

We had a couple of days respite after the Caen assault and stopped in an open field.

Caen had been cleared up to the Canal, but Jerry was still on the other side of the Canal, so we were deployed North West of Caen and did work to assist the advance beyond.

When that had been successfully completed, we returned to Benouville, and were there for several days again. I think it was on the way back that I saw some people looking at their damaged house. Two ladies, about 45 years old, were crying their eyes out and yet not at all bitter towards us. Their house was beyond repair and would have to be completely rebuilt.

From our Water Tower observation post in the grounds of the Maternity Home, we were able to watch the 8000 tons bombing raid on Caen and the terrific artillery barrage that took place at the same time. Things were about to change.

As previously mentioned, we made friends with some of the Maternity Home staff. We stayed there many days, during which my French improved considerably. One evening we were informed that the next day we would be leaving Benouville, and taking up new positions because of the progress in the battle around Caen. The girls and the one man came to us for a farewell "party". There was plenty of talking and then some singing. For some English songs there was a French version so these were sung together in the two languages. We listened to them singing some of their French songs to us, and then we responded with "Land of Hope and Glory", "There's a long long trail awinding" and, of course, our respective National Anthems. The very last song was Auld Lang Syne with versions in both languages. The party broke up with many tears and promises to write to each other.

In the morning I had to go out with a party to reel in telephone wire and it was almost time to depart when we got back. So off we dashed to say goodbye and they left their work and came down to the truck to see us off. There were a lot of promises to write, etc. and then time was up. Bobby was saying goodbye to his Daisy (yes she was French) and me to my Therese. She kissed me goodbye and then hurried away for about 12 yards, then turned into the hedge bitterly sobbing. She had to wait for Andree to escort her up. If I had gone to her, it would only have prolonged the agony. I noticed Daisy had tears down her cheeks even before she turned away. They were good friends indeed. There were two fellows whose friends couldn't leave the Hospital area so they went up for a quick goodbye. On their way to the truck they passed the returning Daisy, Therese and Andree, the two former still crying.

We had by this time driven Jerry from across the River and the Canal so we advanced to Honorine et Chauderette (Spelling might be a little askew). Here we were in an orchard surrounded by high trees (and also by notices saying there were booby traps around). We had to dig it and make dugouts. Believe me they were lovely. Mine had cupboards built into one side, a gauze window, and mosquito - proof doorway. The walls were lined with lead and we slept on chestnut paling covered with a thick mattress. This was a rather 'hot' spot (i.e from enemy shelling) but we thoroughly enjoyed it all. We must have raided some derelict properties to get the materials to make those dugouts !

Our Battery Commander, Major Humphrey, was said to be hopeless at reading maps. In the first month of the campaign, he three times ordered troops into areas in no-mans-land, in front of the front line infantry! This once necessitated a two mile retreat to get back to the Commune of Fountaine - Henry, safe in Allied hands.

Someone wrote a song about this episode and it was later sung at army concerts. I can't remember the whole song but we all remembered the last line "On to Fountaine-Henry where no one's been before".

Major Humphrey was later awarded an MBE.

An incident occured when I was seconds from death. I was walking across a road when my sergeant shouted to me and, with his arms outstretched indicated that enemy planes were approaching. They started machine gun fire along the line of the road as I dived into a roadside ditch, just in time because the bullets immediately hit the road three feet in front of me, exactly where I had been those couple of seconds earlier.

Later a strange throbbing sound became louder and louder and then cut out - I didn't know it then, but it was a V1 Flying Bomb which had lost its way. It turned and went back in the direction from which it had come and, as a result, exploded in enemy territory.

"One day we were surprised to find the girls came up for a short visit on bicycles." Goodness knows how they found out where we were stationed. It was a very short visit because, at that time, we were very busy with our military operations.

As we advanced slowly against stiff resistance as a part of the battle to secure Caen, we got to a damaged building that had formally been a post office. It was at a cross roads, quite high up and overlooked the land still in enemy control. We quickly got set up to start searching for targets. A tank battle started up on the upward sloping ground just under a mile away, and we were able to monitor and report on the progress.

After a while, Field Marshall Montgomery came and stopped right beside the house and was himself watching the tank battle that was under way. He had with him a motor cycle escort. We were carefully disguising the fact that we were there and along comes Monty and his retinue in full view of the enemy! They didn't stay long but had obviously been spotted, because we immediately came under heavy mortar fire. I was caught in the open, so ran and lay down between one of our vehicles and the side wall of the building to get some protection from the exploding missiles.

In the fields as we moved around, there was a common sight: cattle, that had been killed by the shell-fire, lying around. Their bodies very soon filled with gas and became very bloated. They were lying on their backs with their legs sticking straight up into the air. Wherever there had been heavy battles, the sight of these bodies in the countryside became very common.

"From St Honorine we went through Caen to Cormelles where we worked for the eventual advance which closed the Falaise Pocket." We took over a brickworks, so had a building to live in and there was a swimming pool there. This area was also used as a base for Tanks. We saw them go out to deploy and then return. One I remember had been on fire. I climbed up on the top of this tank and looked down into the interior. There were two shapes, completely black and featureless that had been the remains of the crew. There was a call for a volunteer to go down into the tank and bring the remains up to be taken away for burial.

The brickwork main building was quite tall, probably about the height of a four storey block of flats. It had a flat roof and on that roof was a small structure housing a lift motor. We set up our observation post in this structure because of its height, and the fact that from inside we had a clear view of the area controlled by the enemy. I was on duty there when we were asked to monitor the position of bombs to be dropped by a major air strike. I saw a large number of planes coming in our direction and, as they reached where we were, there was a huge explosion very near to me. I was wearing a telephone headset as I was reporting by wire. This was torn from my head and I was sucked out of the building and landed on the tarmac flat roof outside. I remember that very close to where I landed there was a large piece of bomb casing, half buried in the tarmac roofing and sizzling away.

The pathfinder plane which had the task of pinpointing the target for the following bombers, had mistakenly identified the Polish Armoured Unit as being German, and directed the bombers to that spot. Our position was adjacent to the Poles who were waiting to take action to close the Falaise Gap.

The second wave of planes had been instructed to drop their bombs into the smoke caused by the first wave's bombs. Our Forces could not identify the wireless wavelength of the incoming planes, so a Typhoon fighter plane was scrambled and sent to divert them. He got to them and repeatedly dipped one wing and then the other in quick succession in front of this second wave of planes, but they didn't realise what was going on, until the Typhoon opened fire on the leading plane so blew off its tail. They then realised that something was amiss so turned and retreated. I expect the pilot of the Typhoon was also drawing close and waving frantically to the leading plane's crew. These were American planes. The crew of the shot down plane baled out and, when they landed, had to be taken into custody to be interviewed. I understood that one of them landed very near to one of our O.Ps (Observation Posts) so they had the job of taking that American back to our Headquarters Unit.

About this time I had a letter from home which told me that a Mr. Williams was writing, presumably in a newspaper, that the French people were complaining about the bombing that had been taking place.

I wrote back "You can take it from me that what Mr. Williams was writing about the French people is absolutely wrong. Every single person that I have spoken to about our bombing and shelling (and it's several) are sorry that French lives are lost but admit that it was, and is, all very necessary. I've been in the company of some of them when dreadful barrages and heavy raids are in progress and they literally jump for joy. A batch of Jerry prisoners were being marched along the road one day and a man could hold himself no longer and lashed out at a couple of them. The guard told him to stop as he would never help matters in that way".

We had to move around quite a lot before capturing Caen and this included two days rest at Douvres les Deliverandes. We passed through Blainville, on to Ouistreham and even had a swim at Luc sur Mere and Lion sur Mere. In the midst of our military activities we had one day's rest at Gazelle. We also stopped over at Mondeville and passed through Bievelle.

Time had moved on and the following extract is from a letter I wrote home on 29th October 1944.

It starts off by saying that I hoped that Dad's cold was much better as he had had it too long.

Then

"It's a pity we can't send home an unlimited amount of goods, at least not without Duty, or else I could have easily got you an alarm clock. The shops out here on the Marks and Spencer lines have them piled up on the counters just like in peacetime. There is also no shortage of wrist watches here at prices ranging from 600 francs (Approx. £3.15.0) and pocket watches from about 500 francs (£2.10.0) Don't get the idea that because of this there are no shortages out here. Jerry couldn't work the systems as well as we did at home. There are these luxuries out here but food is not plentiful; in England it was better no luxuries but ample food. Anyway I expect Jerry ran the black market so it didn't pay him to organise things any other way.

FLASH. I know a little boy in Northern France who killed two Germans by borrowing (without the owner's knowledge) a Gendarme's revolver. His age? - about ten."

That letter then goes on to explain that Duty Free labels had just been issued and detailed the contents of a parcel I was sending home and who the various items were intended for.

After leaving the brickworks at Cormelles, it was almost a case of trying to keep up with the Germans, they were being beaten back so quickly and so far. This meant that during this period all we could do was to keep up with the front line as far as possible, but had little time to set up observation posts and use our location skills.

As the front line moved beyond Le Havre, the garrison there was completely cut off from the rest of the German forces. Le Havre was completely encircled and there was no way by which the Germans could escape the entrapment and join their main forces. As a result, we were called back to help with the elimination of this pocket of resistance. A map of this area is included (Page 48).

At the top of the cliff overlooking the town there was a large chateau named Chateau Gonfreville l'Orcher. There was an open paved area in front of the chateau and across from the main building was a row of garages, stores, etc. We decided to occupy these, and, as we were obviously going to be there for several days, unloaded all our equipment. Just below the top of the cliff there was a ledge which was a perfect location for observations. We quickly got our instrument, telephone equipment, etc. into position and camouflaged it to avoid being spotted by the Germans below. Yes, as well as being in the town, and in the docks area, they were actually in the road immediately below where

we were located. The German army had been there before us because there was some of their equipment left behind, due to the speed in which they had left the chateau and retreated down to the town. There was a crate of German rifles and a lot of ammunition. We couldn't resist playing with these. We were taking potshots at glass insulators on pylons, part of the Schneider Aircraft works (so we understood). The Germans had noticed this activity and wondered what was going on. At nightfall, the men at our observation post reported that there was movement in the woods just beyond the post. We quickly grabbed rifles, sten guns, etc. and slowly and quietly went into the woods, but they must have heard our activity and withdrew. They didn't try a repeat visit.

Ever since being a young boy I have had an interest in medical things. In fact, all I ever wanted to be was a Surgeon, in particular a Plastic Surgeon. Whilst most kids of my age were reading comics, some of my reading material was concerned with this interest. The result of this interest was that I stood in for our Troop's Medical Orderly when he went on leave. With me on the continent, I always had a supply of medical essentials.

The Chateau was occupied by a lot of civilians that had come out there to escape the fighting in Le Havre itself. On the first day there was someone there who had cut themselves, so out came the first-aid kit and I cleaned and dressed the wound. On the second day that we were there, I saw a little girl who was suffering from malnutrition and had the telltale sores on her body. I called her over and treated the sores with Acriflavine cream and gave her a supply of vitamin tablets. That really started something. From then on, every day there was a queue to see 'the doctor'- Me!

I was able to arrange my army observation duties in such a way that it was possible each day to start my 'clinic' at half past ten until midday and then stop for a meal break.

We soon had people coming up from a nearby village asking to see the Doctor. There were so many that needed attention that I enlisted the help of a couple of my colleagues who were interested in helping. I would decide what treatment was necessary, and pass on routine things to them.

We had an elderly man come to us, who had a very severe shrapnel wound that had almost severed his arm. I knew that there was a Military Forward Hospital Unit very near to us, so I transported the man to them for treatment that I could not possibly give. At the Unit they said to me "We will supply you with anything you need and you can bring to us anyone you decide needs our facilities".

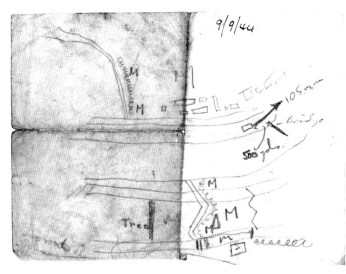

9/9/44

◀ **Plate 5**
Sketch of enemy
locations made
whilst looking down
from a cliff-top
position. Our
Observation Post
was on the cliff top
directly above these
defenses.

▶ **Plate 6**
Notes made with
the help of a
young French
man whilst
spying on the
enemy defences
of Le Havre"

LE HAVRE   9/9/44.

Germans occupying buildings
a line from MR. 558269 to MR. 564267
concrete also structure holding
105mm gun at M.R. 557270
Germans occupying building
(possibly blockhouse) at M.R. 568 274
manning barricade across the road.
Another barricade approx 200' yds.
towards Le Havre, area between
is mined.

Detailed mine map tomorrow.

Blockhouse also (by information only).
at MR544277 and 545274
Canon approx. 37 m.m. at large
Barrage.

A mother brought along a little baby covered all over in sores which I assumed to be eczema, but it could have been the result of venereal disease infection. I passed them on to a nearby Red-Cross station.

Just after that, a victim of a cycle accident was brought to me, but this girl was quite badly injured so I decided to get her to the hospital unit without delay. She was admitted and kept in the hospital for a week

This went on all the days we were there and when we were eventually leaving, that first little girl came running up to me to give me a card from her missal as a 'thank you' present.

One of my 'patients' was a very attractive blonde nineteen or twenty years old. She was one of the many suffering from malnutrition. The next day she came back and brought her older brother with her. They had come from an area which was considered as enemy territory. Whether they took a chance in coming to us or whether the Germans actually permitted them to come, I just don't know.

This young man seemed completely genuine so I took a chance on him not being there to betray me and went a little way along the cliff top to where we had a view of the ground below our post. He was pointing out to me where the German defences were located, mined areas, barbed wire fences, the occupied blockhouse, etc. I made a sketch of all this on the back of a letter I had in my pocket (Plate 5). I see I dated it 9.9.44. Attached also are the notes I made at the time, also dated, of course, 9.9.44 (plate 6).

The Germans seemed to be careless in regard to exposing their positions. One day I watched a team setting up a mobile anti-aircraft gun at one of the docks. It was quite easy for me to map-read this location and pass it back to H.Q. so that they could inform our artillery of a target. I believe it was destroyed.

It seems strange now to talk in these terms, but I considered I had one of my most successful observation results at this location. I saw a very heavy anti-aircraft battery open up on some of our planes as they approached. I very soon had their exact position passed back to Corps and they brought air-burst shell fire on to the exact position. I expect the gun crew were killed or wounded, as they did not fire again. I see it now as being a sad reflection of the degrading effect of war involvement when, in explaining this incident to my parents I wrote

"I hope that several of them died like the cornered rats they were, in any case I'll bet the bomber crews were glad they stopped firing".

51

But there you are, that's war.

The Garrison Commander was instructed to surrender to avoid a battle, but he refused more than once. In the end he was told that if he didn't surrender, that night a thousand bomber raid would be launched on Le Havre. Again he refused to give in.

That night there was a bombing raid on the town, but it was not the threatened thousand bomber raid. This raid was to enable us to pinpoint his anti-aircraft gun positions and so that when the real raid came in the next night, we opened up fire on the located positions, and I believe I said at the time that only one of their guns was firing, and that was probably a mobile gun which had not fired in that position the previous night.

The garrison did then surrender and I have a memory of the German soldiers marching up the road from the town in order to surrender as prisoners of war, but you would have thought they were on a military demonstration. They were determined not to look disheartened and came out looking proud.

After dealing with Le Havre, we moved forward again to catch up with the latest battle situations. It was a case of setting up and then moving on again, not able to use our role as observers, other than on odd occasions. It was a case of following the advances and being available. We passed in the vicinity of Lisieux, Pont Audemer, Albert, and Arras. I saw, at Albert, the religious statue on the top of a church. My Dad had described to me how it had been damaged in the First World War and was hanging upside down. It was said at the time that if the statue fell, we would lose the war. Somewhere in that area my father received severe injuries from a grenade and was left on the battlefield as being dead. A retreating soldier noticed my father move and stopped to pick him up and carry him back to get medical treatment. But for that unknown soldier's action, I would not be here!

As we entered Belgium we came to a little village named Baal, just South of Lier. We weren't lucky enough to get billets as was usual in those days, so we had to pitch our tent. Right after that we had to attend a parade for the purpose of changing our French money into Belgian money. My colleague, Ron, and I walked into the village, which meant that we were the first troops they had seen after the fighting in that area. Two little girls came rushing up to us and gave each of us a huge peach. We continued up through the main street, obviously the centre of attention, as these people were seeing their liberators for the first time. There were two girls and an old man talking away. We stopped and tried to converse with them in a mixture of French, English and Flemish. Very soon we were surrounded by the locals and someone took us home for supper, and I wrote home to say that it was much enjoyed - a change from routine army food. We were invited to return the next day when a local festival had been organised. There was a fair in the village square, dancing and music all over the place. In that letter home, I explained that we had fruit tart, bread and butter and coffee. It started to rain and the people were annoyed because they wanted us to pose for them to take photographs.

We passed through or in the vicinity of Tournai, Brussels, and Antwerp, and stopped in the village of Westmalle. A letter my parents received, from a girl in the village of Westmalle, records that we stayed for eight days in their village. I remember we set up a tent (a posh name for a rig-up of a large tarpaulin over a framework of poles) on the lawn of one of the houses. The local people were so appreciative of being liberated that they were always trying to say 'Thank you' in various ways. In particular there was an endless supply of peaches - far more than we could eat. One young girl could speak a little English and saw me as her friend. She took me home to meet her family. They were the owners of the village shop. I don't know the date when this took place, but some time afterwards my parents received that letter (Plates 7-10).

Someone attempted a translation for them which reads as follows:

"A few reconnaissance to out English savers.

Dear family Cole,

I see already that it is a big surprise to receive a few words in French from a small daughter of Belgium.

Your dear son, Norman was at our home for 8 days and I found that he is a good soldier with a good, very good character. I think also to those parents who are so far away from their big son and I see that I am obliged to write a few words to the parents of courage which . . . . To go out to their big Norman and do not know when he will return.

Mr. and Mrs. Do not think that I am forced to write something, Oh no, for I also have good parents and 2 little sisters. If it is not asking too much of you, I would like to receive a small letter from you dear English friend.

Again a time our very, very good compliments to all our English savers.

Papa, Marys, Julia and Jeanne"

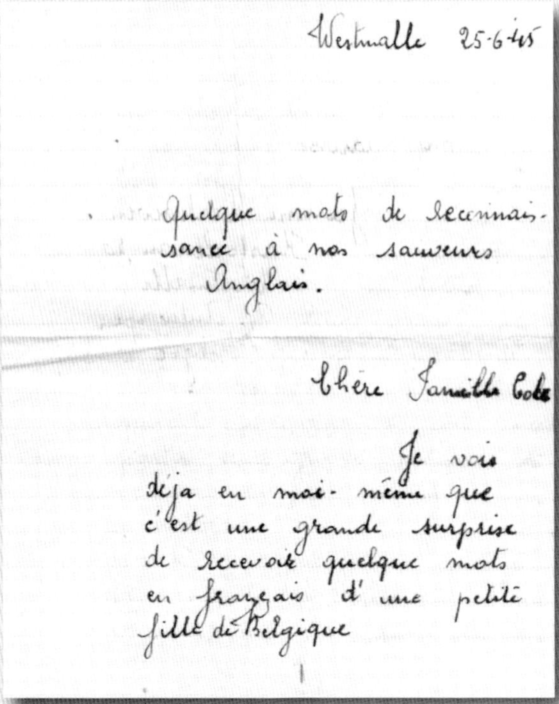

Westmalle 25·6·45

◄ **Plate7**

Quelque mots de reconnaissance à nos sauveurs
Anglais.

Chère Famille Cole

Je vois
déja en moi-même que
c'est une grande surprise
de recevoir quelque mots
en frazçais d'une petite
fille de Belgique

▶ **Plate8**

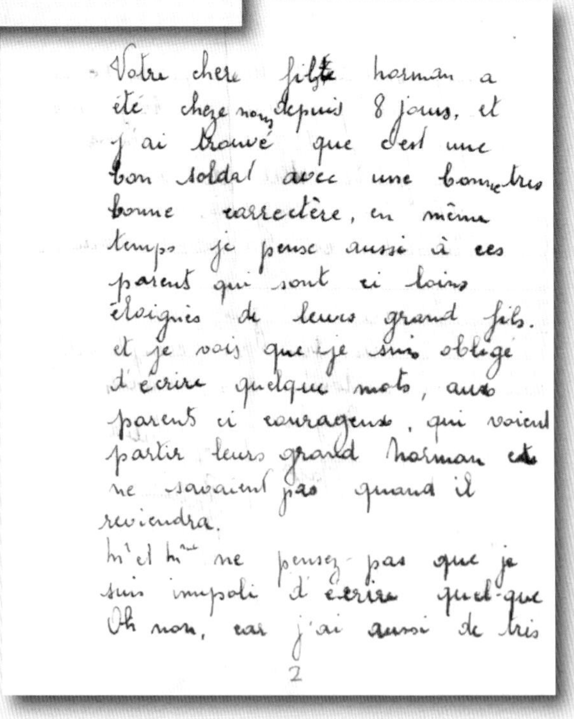

Votre chere fille Norman a
été chez nous depuis 8 jours, et
j'ai trouvé que c'est une
bon soldat avec une bonne très
bonne carrectère, en même
temps je pense aussi à ces
parents qui sont si loins
éloignés de leurs grand fils.
et je vois que je suis obligé
d'écrire quelque mots, aux
parents si courageux, qui voient
partir leurs grand Norman et
ne savaient pas quand il
reviendra.
Mr et Mme ne pensez pas que je
suis impoli d'écrire quelque
Oh non, car j'ai aussi de très

2

54

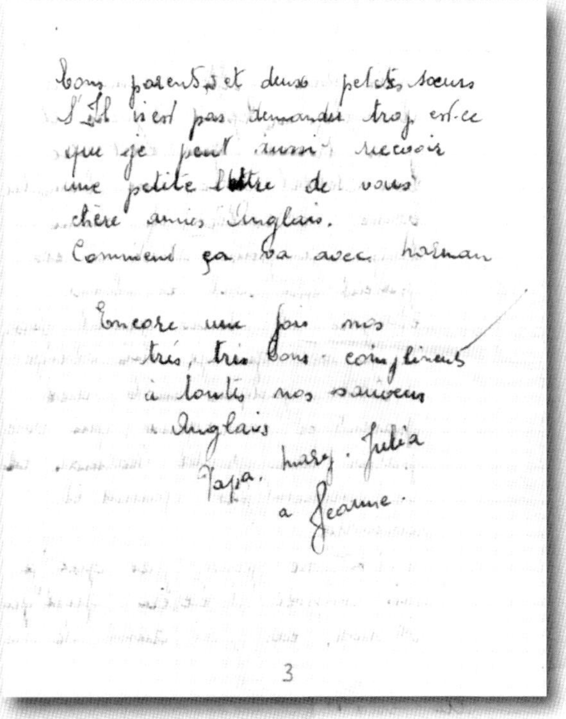

bon, parents et deux petites soeurs
S'il n'est pas demandé trop est-ce
que je peut aussi recevoir
une petite lettre de vous
chère amies Anglais.
Comment ça va avec maman

Encore une fois mes
très, très bons compliment
à toutes nos sauveurs
Anglais
Papa, Mary, Julia
a Jeanne.

3

◀ Plate9

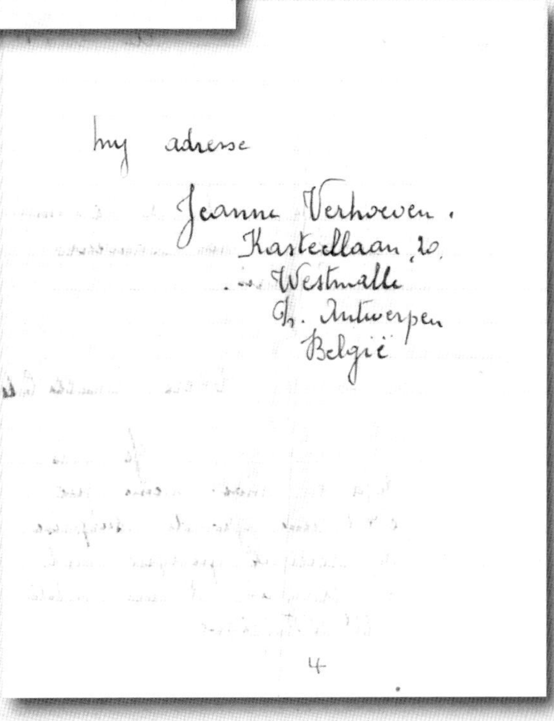

▶ Plate10

my adresse

Jeanne Verhoeven.
Kasteellaan 20.
Westmalle
Ch. Antwerpen
België

4

▲ Flashspotting Troop of the 9th Survey Regiment R.A. at Tilburg

▲ "A" Post of the Flashspotting Troop. I am seated second from the left

Not good English and perhaps not a very accurate translation, but that was how it was translated by someone for my parents, who knew no French. Whether they did reply, I do not know. It was towards the end of October 1944 when we entered Westmalle. As we were leaving that village, the little girl came running up to me and gave me a penknife with a picture of Westmalle on the handle. As far as I know I don't have it now.

I walked into a village which we had just captured after very heavy shelling. The village was in ruins but on the side of the road was what looked like an almost new British army steel helmet - much more presentable than mine. I thought "I'll have that one in place of my present one." I picked it up but quickly dropped it again. Inside was a large part of the owner's head. It had obviously received the blast from a near-miss shell which had decapitated the poor lad. This must have been blown some distance through the air because there was no sign of the rest of the body nearby.

We were advancing along a road when we noticed a flotilla of bombers approaching us. We were up close to the German's positions and that could have been their targets. Suddenly we recognised that the bombs were dropping short, in fact, right where we were. Fortunately for us the road ran alongside a railway line and we were just where the line emerged from a tunnel. We abandoned everything and rushed into the tunnel for protection. The bombing continued for a while but we were safe and sound and I'm sure our vehicles, etc. received no damage.

We advanced to a front line position which was a road that ran from left to right in front of us. We held the one side and over the road was a wood in which were the Germans. Just short of the road was a church and we decided to use the tower as an observation point. A column of infantry went past us up to the road and into the woods. We were thinking 'rather them than us' going into that wood looking for a fight. After a while they returned and they were saying to us, "we wouldn't fancy going up a tower like that because if the Germans get back, you are trapped." Each of us saw the other's role as the more dangerous. We drew back a little way and stopped near a farmhouse. Whilst we were there we were surprised to see a few German soldiers approaching holding surrender leaflets, and instead of coming to us, they went across the open ground to where there was a barbed wire enclosed store of precast concrete, and settled down inside awaiting collection. To them it seemed natural that, because they were now prisoners of war, they would naturally be behind barbed wire.

In Antwerp there was more than one NAAFI canteen, and I wrote home to say that I had bought in one of them, a souvenir which I was sending home. The letter then goes on to describe these canteens in the following words:

"In England a NAAFI is usually a wood or tin building with a rough and ready serving bar. Out here it's different. The NAAFI in the Grand Hotel was taken over with all its staff and a smashing orchestra. It's an absolutely super hotel. You go in, sit at a table and a waiter comes up and gets your order and what's more I should think that there's a waiter to about every four or five tables.

There is another NAAFI, The Antwerp Arms. This is a large hotel with a huge bar lounge on the ground floor and a nice dining room with an all round balcony and another nice orchestra. There is a YMCA (Young Men's Christian Association) in the square, another large hotel, but they have only taken over part of it. The Salvation Army was the first one to open and again they're in a terrific hotel, really smart and modern. There is a NAAFI Cinema and a NAAFI Theatre and it's in the latter that I've seen all the shows I've spoken about."

Due to the fact that there was only very limited military activity at this time in this area, we were able to have these one day breaks.

I had seen women with shaved heads being paraded around to shame them for having befriended the Germans, but in a zoo (and I can't remember whether it was Antwerp or Brussels) I walked between the animal cages, but instead of animals, those who had collaborated with the occupiers were on display to the public as traitors.

As we advanced we passed through Breda and settled into an unoccupied school in Tilburgh. It was to be our base for several weeks.

An airborne assault by the British Forces now known as the Battle for Arnhem (Operation Market Garden) took place on the 17th September 1944. The British 30 Corps, supported by the 1st Corps, were despatched across Holland to link up with the airborne forces, who should have secured a bridge over the River Rhine, but in fact were unable to do so. I was part of the 1st Corps troops involved in that operation.

We travelled to a position near Nijmegen on the road to Arnhem, but we were instructed to get clear of the main, rather narrow, road to enable the tanks to move forward; they were needed in an attempt to break through the German front line. They were beaten back and could not get through to relieve the encircled airborne forces. We made no further progress and had to pull back into South Holland.

It is interesting that, at a later date we were to cross that bridge, but it was still under fire from the enemy. To minimise the chance of being targeted, Military Police lined up a few vehicles at a time, a short distance from the bridge. We were told to get up speed as we approached the bridge, so that by the time we were crossing we did so at speed and were over as quickly as possible. Although the bridge was under enemy observation, we did not get fired on, and afterwards we returned to Tilburg.

The front line had settled on the River Maas, the British on the South bank and the Germans held the North side. This became a stalemate. There was, of course, a lot of mortar and artillery shelling, but no attempts to cross the river. Our arrangement was for some of our troops to be at the river bank for a few days and then return to be replaced by fresh colleagues. At night, it was like a firework display to the sides and in front of us, because so many tracer bullets and flare shells were being used.

One day I was outside the school and got talking to a young (?16 year old) girl, whose name was Adri. She was learning English at her school, so we were able to converse, albeit it with some difficulty. She took me to her home and introduced me to her parents, elder sister and two younger brothers. They became like a personal family to me and Adri and I became very close friends - she had a lovely personality. The two boys were mad about their English soldier friend and would cling to me all the time. There was also an older brother, Frans, that I met later.

I have often wondered how the relationship between Adri and myself would have developed in different circumstances. There is no doubt that at that time I had fallen in love with Adri. It was reciprocated and on the back of the photograph of herself with Tonny and little Louis, Adri had written "For the sweetest boy in the world. With my love, Adri."

In those days there was little tolerance between the Roman Catholic church and the Evangelical churches. Adri was part of a very strict Roman Catholic family whereas my background was evangelical. I know that at the time I feared that this could prove to be a barrier to any permanent relationship between us.

I knew I would be moving on from Tilburg and getting involved in military action. I suppose the thoughts of a permanent relationship with Adri slowly faded, as time and distance separated us. The strange thing is that in due course I came back home and married my dear wife Mary, notwithstanding the fact

▲ Photo of the Van den Brekel family. Little Leo who was killed is the boy in the front centre position. Adri is the young lady on the extreme left.

▶ In this smaller photograph Adri is on the right and her little brother, Louis, is on the left.

I think it might be Adri's sister Tonny in the middle but I am not sure.

that she too was an ardent Roman Catholic when I met her - but that is a full story in itself!

An emergency situation arose. We had a message to say that an attack by a German parachute regiment was probable. The Herman Goering Parachute Regiment had arrived on their side of the river. I have a clear memory of taking a few of our Troop and carrying out a reconnaissance around the perimeter of the school premises, carefully peering around each corner in case the parachutists had landed. We had to have loaded rifles with us at all times, and the engines of our vehicles had to be started up at regular intervals, to keep them warm and ready for an emergency retreat if the parachute attack took place. It never did.

One day I took one of our motor cycles and went out to the town to try and arrange a football match with a local team. Whether I succeeded or not I am not sure, but the thing that puzzles me is why I took a motor bike, I hated riding them. Why didn't I take a Jeep instead?

Another sporting moment: we had an approach from a local hockey team to ask if we could raise a team to give them some practice. We did so, and I was one of the players - I had never played hockey in my life. I don't remember the game, but I do remember that it was reported locally that that Tilburgh hockey team had played a game against England! So I can say that I have played hockey for England!

I had to do a journey in a post truck. You would never believe so much could happen to one vehicle in so short a time. A run of bad luck wasn't in it. To start with, the water in the radiator started to steam so we stopped to find out what was wrong. We found that the pump that circulates the water was faulty. We decided to journey on slowly, but the engine wouldn't start again. The petrol pump had gone 'phut'. We put that right and, in doing so, got an air-lock in the petrol pipes. We decided we'd had enough so decided to have a tow to the journey's end. Our troubles were not over though - the tow-bar snapped in half. After much effort we got the engine ticking over slowly and started on our journey. I suppose we'd been going for about five minutes when the battery stopped charging. We pulled up immediately and found that water was pouring out of the radiator bottom. The fan belt had broken, opened a water tap and that also meant that the batteries were not being charged. After all this we managed to get hold of a new fan belt and finish the journey.

It was now the 21st February 1945. I wrote the following letter to my parents:

*"Please excuse the bad scribbling but I've just had a big shock I
was able this evening to get to Adri's house and on arrival here
was told that the second younger brother had been killed by
what I cannot say (it was a German bomb). Believe me these
people here are every bit as family loving as you and Dad and
the loss of this boy means the same to them as it would have to
you if it was me. Only last night I was in this very room
playing with him so you guess what a shock I had when this
news greeted me. I have today written an application for
permission to attend the funeral and will let you know if this is
granted or not.*

*Please pass a message into the first church meeting that you
attend and ask them all to pray for Mr. and Mrs. van den Brekel
and family - remember after all this time, it's like my own
family. I shall be praying plenty for them myself. It is very
difficult here for me as I can't speak to them enough to say all
the things I would like to. ....One of the embarrassing things that
I had to do immediately I came in was to see the collection of all
the photos in which he is featured. ... I've just had a look at a
drawing of Christ wearing the crown of thorns and as soon as he
(Leo) had done it he told his mother to show it to me, he was so
proud of it. Both of these boys would do anything to see me for a
few minutes, and used to cry when told that I had to go away or
if I was staying, that they had to go to bed. As a matter of fact
only a minute or so before his death he was asking his mother to
give a shout immediately I arrived. He was hoping that I would
turn up early in the afternoon instead of in the evening as
normal. It was not easy sitting with Mum on the point of
collapse, Adri and Tonny (her sister) breaking down
occasionally and every so often a tear rolling down the cheeks of
both Dad and Frans, the eldest brother."*

The following day I went to Adri's house , I expect she was at school. Tonny
and her fiance took me along to the hospital to see Leo. He was to be buried the
following day but it is the rule that the parents see him the day previous. Whilst
we were there a Sister came and they intoned a prayer of some kind. He was

all prepared for this to take place - a little white sheet was neatly folded so that only his hands and face were showing. Toni was alright for a couple of minutes and then she broke down. She knelt on one knee beside the coffin, put her hand on his crossed hands and kept kissing him, quietly murmuring his name all the while.

On the day of the funeral I had to be at the house by a quarter to nine in the morning. When I arrived, there was only the family, but very soon relatives started to arrive and at a quarter to ten we all set off for the church. There were seven people killed as well as Leo, so in the church we had front seats in groups. The service didn't mean much to me, as I couldn't understand the language and I didn't know the Catholic form of service. It was very touching and the singing was lovely. After the service the men only went to the cemetery and the women returned to the house.

The cortege order was this. First were Leo's schoolmates, the hearse (drawn by a horse covered with a black cloth), and then us, walking in single file. Behind us were the other hearses followed by their mourners. At the graveside the children sang some really lovely pieces. I remember standing for a moment and saluting Leo's coffin as a sign of respect for his life.

From the cemetery we walked back to the house, this time in pairs, and there the ladies had coffee waiting for us. Slowly the relatives drifted away until just the immediate family was left.

There was one very touching incident. In the church , the mother of one child whose coffin was laid in line with the others, stood quietly. She was a person about thirty years old, and was alright as long as she could see the coffin but, as they picked it up and carried it down the aisle, she started to shout out his name at the top of her voice and then just collapsed across the pew in front of her.

The story behind this is that an armoured column of the Canadian army had entered Tilburgh and, in an attempt to hide them, had dispersed their tanks in the streets . Little Leo had been sent by his mother to buy a loaf from the nearby shop when the bombs dropped. Mrs. Van den Brekel ran out and found Leo badly injured, and cradled him in her arms as he was dying.

I have three cards (Plates 11-13), the one with details of all the persons killed along with the one showing St Joseph were given out at the church (12 & 13), the one which refers to Leo alone, was given to me by his family(11).

◀ Plate 11

A card produced by the Van den Brekel family in memory of their son, Leo, killed as the result of enemy action.

▲ A translation of Leo's card

In memory of Leo van den Brekel.

Mass Server of the Parish Church, Gashouse Street, born in Tilburg 18th Nov. 1933 and involved in the war tragedy of the 21st Feb. '45.

He was on his way to do an errand for his mother when this happy lad was knocked down by the violence of war and died instantly in the arms of his mother. We mankind cannot understand what God meant by that, that He took this boy from the love and care of his parents. But we know in and through our Holy intuition that what God does for us is the best. He had been elected for a holy work, to serve the priest at Mass, now he may serve as an angel and follow the Lamb of God in Heaven. My dear Father & Mother, you cared for me a lot but from this care that you so willingly gave for me, our Lord has liberated you. Your duty is finished.

I have reached my aim in life which God entrusted to me and now I take care of you, and will carry your prayers to God.

My dear little brother & sisters, you must try by your righteousness & love to fill the empty place I have left, for one another and for Father & Mother.

There is an empty place in my family caused by my death.

Holy Tarcisius, patron of Mass Servers, pray for us.

A translation of the card distributed at the Church:-

(List of all the victims names here)

Who so unexpectedly became victims of the war tragedy of 21/2/45 and were wrenched from our midst. Let us always remember them in Holy Mass and in our Prayers.

The dead of the righteous are precious in God's sight. Holy Jopseph, patron of the good dead, I have my trust in you.

I'm no poet but I wrote the following poem at the time:

When I first was invited to come to your house,
I had doubts as to the welcome I'd get,
These soon were dispelled, I learnt very soon,
They're the best folks I could possibly have met.

For months I've been with you, and your home is mine,
You were just as a brother to my mind,
And now you've been taken, the blow has been hard,
Fate seems to have been very unkind.

I shall always remember you, could I ever forget,
I shall picture you playing at Christ's feet,
One day too all my trials will be over,
And once more in Heaven we'll meet.

From Tilburgh we were sent to an island in the south west corner of Holland, North Beveland. There were only two towns there and we were deployed in one of them, Wissekerke, for a few days. There didn't have to be any fighting, because the Germans had fled from the islands before we got there.

The people there were very fond of their national costume, the ladies with light blue and white clothes and those 'butterfly' hats and the men with their baggy trousers. Even the very young children were togged up in similar costume (Plates 14-17).

We were billeted in civvie's houses in pairs. A colleague, Ron, and I were housed in a farmhouse. A daughter there spoke a little English, so that helped quite a lot. The little bits of Dutch that we had picked up were not much use as they spoke with an entirely different accent. We watched the ladies producing lace by using only their fingers.

A quote from my letter to home, dated 13th March 1945:

"There is one funny incident that I must tell you about. It concerns 'cook' Cole ! Never knew I'd been on a cook's course did you? I haven't either but I had a 'do' at cooking the other day mind you, I didn't have much choice in the matter. The other morning we had a bath parade and both the fellows who do our cooking normally, went on it. It left myself and a signaller here to do the dinner and believe me we did 'do' it. There was meat to be roasted, that was o.k., tinned peas, that also o.k. but there were no potatoes. At first we were in a proper 'stew', and then we

De dood van den rechtvaardiger is
kostbaar voor de oogen van God.
(Ps. CXV. 6)

Heilige Jozef, patroon van
den goeden dood, ik
heb vertrouwen op U.

W. W. H   N° 25

◀ **Plate 12**

Cards issued by the Parish Church
of Tilburgh in memory of those killed
by a bomb on the 21st February 1945.

▼ **Plate 13**

✝ Parochie Gasthuisstraat
Tilburg

IN PACE CHRISTI

Parochianen, laten wij onze mede-parochianen

Michaël Zebregts
geb. 2 Februari 1881

Maria In 't Ven-van de Pol
geb. 20 Maart 1885

Cornelia Cools
geb. 7 September 1910

Jan van Loon
geb. 30 October 1932

Leo van den Brekel
geb. 18 November 1933

Rudolf van Lent
geb. 7 Maart 1934

Willy van Berendonk
geb. 13 December 1936

die zoo onverwachts als slachtoffers van de
oorlogsramp van 21 Februari 1945 uit ons
midden werden weggerukt, in onze gebeden
en heilige Misoffers blijven gedenken.

had a brainwave. We would make dumplings. We got out all the ingredients that we thought went into the making of dumplings and started mixing. Flour, fat, a little milk and a pinch of both salt and baking powder - then some water for mixing purposes.

After much kneading we rolled the mixture into balls and put them into boiling water. At dinner time we expected them to have collapsed and to look something like porridge. We weren't half pleased when we saw that they were still in their original shape. We tried them with a knife and ugh! Were they hard, the knife almost broke in two. (We didn't lose on the deal though, we sold them to the local hockey club who were unable to get new balls.)" If you believe what is in the brackets, you'll believe anything. The rest is true.

All this time I was having to take my turn up on the banks of the River Maas, as this was still the fighting front line. Away to our right there was an island in the middle of the river, and it was occupied by the Germans. It was decided to drive the Germans from this position. There had been a snowfall. The infantry came along all clothed in white, their rifles wrapped in white material, and they had amphibian tanks all painted white. There was a lot of shell fire and presumably the infantry and tanks made their attack, but the outcome was that the Germans were still there - I believe it was a S.S. unit.

I was instructed to take a 15 cwt. truck and two drivers to a supply depot to collect another truck. When we got there, a soldier took me to where the vehicle was, handed it over to me and I signed for it. The soldier was a Warrant Officer and he said to me "Now let's go and get yours". I said that I had only come to collect one truck but he insisted there was another one that I had to take back to my unit.

I was astounded when I saw what I was expected to drive back to Tilburg - it was a M14 half-tracked armoured vehicle. I had never driven one or anything like it.

The Sergeant Major said "This is a lovely vehicle, I tuned it myself". He then got into the driver's seat and started the engine. I wouldn't ever have guessed the secret of getting the engine started. The clutch pedal was the starter, until the engine fired, and then it had the normal function of a clutch. After that I had to drive this thing some seventy miles back to my unit. Normally you can tell when to change gear by the sound of the engine, but the noise from the tracks made that impossible. It was a case of quickly learning to gear change by timing. I managed to get it back without damaging it !

Zuid-Beveland

Het Buurpraatje

▲ Plate 14

▼ Plate 15

ZUID-BEVELAND   KLEEDERDRACHTEN ZEELAND

One day the town of Tilburgh had a liberation celebration parade. In the morning there was a procession of youth comprising schools, Scouts, etc. The main event took place in the afternoon. There was a large procession, which was reviewed by Princess Juliana. There were people on the Town Hall balcony when I got there and, after a while, they were joined by the Princess. As she appeared there were loud cheers and a band played the National Anthem and a couple of patriotic songs, which had the crowd singing. I had one of the best views possible because I climbed on to the top of a large illuminated road sign.

A letter I wrote on the 20th May 1945 explained that mail censorship had ceased. So from now on I could write about things as they happened and say where we were and what we were doing.

From this letter :

"Now that we have all the restrictions taken off I'll start by telling you that I'm at present doing guards on the banks of the Maas, North of Tilburgh. It's a bit different up here to what it used to be - I've seen thousands of bullets by night and mortars both day and night, fly across here both ways. Nowadays we aren't shooting at Germans but instead are stopping people from sneaking across the river from Northern Holland down to here. The reason for all this is that in Northern Holland there are thousands of Dutch S.S. troops and they know darn well that their number's up so in all probability several will try to get down here and pass off as ordinary civilians. We haven't got hold of any as yet but we have got some civvies, three were caught yesterday. They came up the river on a barge, dived in for a swim then suddenly made for the shore. Earlier in the day a girl had been caught. She wanted our chaps to shoot her through the leg to make sure she wasn't returned.

I've just been in for a quiet swim in one of the canals here and feel quite cool now. I'm actually sitting on a grass bank writing this..

Tomorrow I get 24 hours rest back in Tilburgh and then come up here for a further 48 hours.

...Whilst the V Bomb attacks were going on we were not allowed into Antwerp and so for about three months we were not allowed there. The first time we went there after the ban was lifted, we

backed the truck into a car park which was really a roped off street. We backed right on to a café in the window of which was a large notice "On demande une demoiselle". (A young lady on request). It reminded us of the difference between the Puritanical way of thinking here in Holland and the free thinking of Belgium."

On the 22nd May 1945 we left Tilburgh and Holland and started on our way to Germany.

I was out on a motor bike, arranging a football match for the next day between Fran Van der Brekel's firm and my troop. When I got back to the school where we were billeted, it was to be greeted with the news that we were confined to barracks as we were moving off.

There was a 'spit and polish' parade that afternoon to say "Goodbye" to our Brigadier (Corps Commander R.A.) He told us that we were leaving 1st Corps and going to Germany to work with an A.A. Brigade, which by then had become an Infantry Brigade. As there was no technical work for us, we must all act as infantry, guards, etc.

After the parade we were allowed out of the school about eight o'clock and, needless to say, I made my way to Adri's house to spend my last few hours with them. They were all very sorry that I had to go after knowing them for some eight months. Mother said , in Dutch of course, "We aren't half going to miss you in the evenings. About half past seven I shall look at the clock and say to Adri, Norman must be going to the NAAFI first before coming here." When it came to saying "Goodbye", Mum was alright until she had to shake hands and then she just broke down. I guess they will miss the fun and games we used to have and I of course, am going to miss them an awful lot.

So to the actual journey away from Tilburgh. We went up through Nijmegen and Arnhem and on to a fair sized town, Enschede, a total journey of about 120 miles. We stopped in this town for a while and my colleague and I went to a NAAFI and for a stroll afterwards. We saw things that we hadn't seen for ages. Collaborators were being rounded up just like in the early days of the invasion. Women used to have their hair cut off before being paraded around the town.

We saw two civilians fighting in the street so when we came across a couple of Orange Soldiers (civilian soldiers), we put them on to the fight to break it up.

There was an undamaged bridge over the River Rhine where the enemy had rushed towards the bridge from different directions and there had obviously been utter confusion. There was no way in their scramble to get to the German side of the river, that they could get all their equipment through the bottleneck, the sound bridge (most others had been destroyed by our bombing and shelling). As a result, they just had to abandon their vehicles and a large amount of equipment. Surprisingly it seemed that nearly all the wagons, etc. were horse drawn. I remember, in particular, there was one wagon which had a huge metal container which was partly filled with soup. I've always believed it was still warm but I'm not sure if that was true.

The next day we restarted our journey and within a quarter of an hour were crossing the border between Holland and Germany. The first thing I can remember seeing, just over the border, were an elderly couple working on the land and, much to my shame I shouted out to them "Work you bastards, work". I suppose I was so indoctrinated to hate the Germans that that was an outburst of my feelings. No excuse though.

My mother and father had sent out some newspapers and I had with me as we journeyed, a copy of the Torquay Times. On the borders of the paper's sheets I made notes as we went along. (Extracted from a letter reproduced on page 173)

Osnabruck was the first large German city we came to and boy! What a mess. It was somewhat reminiscent of Caen only just a shade better - there were a few houses standing in odd places. We went right through the main street and residential centres and it was just driving through a lane of debris for a lot of the way. There were quite a lot of people living there and some of the men were still working, pulling down unsafe walls and tidying up further. It wasn't half a lovely sight to see Germans walking through their all but annihilated city; it must have let them know that their planes could never equal the damage ours had done. Cheers for the R.A.F. eh? They did the work in Osnabruck alright.

Roads. I should imagine the Germans have destroyed utterly the main roads leading into the interior because I've never had such a nightmare journey in all my life. At times we were travelling over tracks that it didn't seem possible to get along, but slowly, painfully slowly we made it. Sometimes we had to follow road deviations to a distance of almost ten miles to cross a river about 100 yards across. I should imagine that Jerry has kept his vital roads in good order and let the others look after themselves.

Hills. After being so long in Holland where the highest 'mountain' is a hump back bridge, it was lovely to see hills getting ever nearer and nearer. When we got into the hilly country it looked just like England. Rugged lanes, just like Devon's and very pretty woods everywhere. It certainly is a very pretty country in fact I'd say the prettiest (including England as a whole) I've ever seen.

Costume. I always thought that tyrolean hats (complete with fuzzy brush) were an old national costume accessory, just worn on special occasions. My belief turned out to be a myth. I saw several men dressed in everyday clothing complete with the tyrolean hat. The women's dress here is very nice and colourful and by far the most tasteful I've ever seen. Their frocks are usually a coloured floral design in which red, white and green seemed to predominate. Another version is a plain coloured frock, white or something like pale blue with this bright material in the form of a little pinafore apron. There was one other fairly common type of dress and that was on the style of a gym slip, usually a white blouse with either a pale blue or this flowered material as the slip. All this lovely dressing tends to put the last little touch to the Girls who certainly leave the rest of the continent standing for looks and attractiveness. The girls around here really are smashing and here is the first thing that the soldiers will have to resist.

Attitude of the civvies. They seem to have all different ideas as to how they should react to us, and we are getting absolute contrasts. The average person seems to watch us in a sort of passive manner, even the majority of the children and just standing and staring, and saying and doing nothing as we pass by. I have even seen people weeping as our huge convoy passes along. Presumably they are just thinking of Germany's hopeless position and disgrace of having thousands of troops pouring in to tell you what you can and cannot do. On the other side of the picture, there have been children waving and shouting to us and in one instance even giving the victory sign. I saw a mother holding up a little baby and getting him to wave to the Tommies. A very nice girl, perhaps about 20 years old, stood in a farmhouse door and waved a duster to me giving such a winsome smile. At our first stop (we halt every 2 hours) an old boy walked down past us saying 'Guten tag' to everyone. To all these things we have never even smiled but simply ignored them. To the children it is very hard and also to ignore the old man when he looks up into your face and passes the time of the day. It makes you feel so ignorant and ill mannered - however, it's the only to treat them yet a while I suppose.

Children. Two things in particular struck me about the children, the first was that they were almost all in bare feet, (as were some of the grown-ups, especially those working in the fields). The second is that there really is a lot of blondes among them.

Refugees. Several times I saw large rooms and halls that had been turned into temporary quarters for homeless people and on the roads were quite a lot opf people pulling little handcarts, or else piled up on horse drawn wagons. Quite a lot had piles strapped on to bicycles which they were pushing if too loaded to ride.

Crops. Our road was all the time through the country and you'd never believe the terrific amount of cultivation here. We were for hundreds of miles on end passing huge corn, potato and vegetable fields. All the crops have lanes of tilled earth between each section. This was to prevent the entire crops being burnt if we dropped incendiaries on the fields. Jutting into these fields at very irregular intervals were catholic wayside altars It doesn't seem believable that the people who have committed all these atrocities could have a religion as well, does it ?

Housing. The houses over here are very pretty indeed I expect you've seen photos of German and Austrian houses. Several times we came across housing estates in the course of construction. I never thought they would have enough labour and materials to do this.

The Occupation Troops. The Occupation Troops I've seen so far, all seem to have lovely billets, hotels and the like and are living in the conditions of privileged tourists. Mind you, the guards here are terrible. All this marching up and down, standing at ease

Greetings from liberated Holland
Groeten uit bevrijd Nederland

▼ Plate 17

Greetings from liberated Holland
Groeten uit bevrijd Nederland

▲ Plate 16

with eyes steady, sort of thing I'm glad I don't have to do sentry duties.

Here on this common, we're living in two man tents as it's only a two day's stay and we then move on to our occupation billets. Last night to crown it all I was on guard so was up and about early in the morning. There's no water here so for a wash and a shave I scooped some rainwater from the cab of my truck with a cup and poured it into a wash bowl. Crude but effective, eh?"

We were quickly allotted our accommodation for the foreseeable future. We were settled into a lovely old hotel. Most of my colleagues were in larger rooms, with two or three to each room, but I was the only one in our Battery to have a room to myself. It was about 12 ft x 9ft, with a polished floor, papered walls and a panelled ceiling There were two windows looking out over the main square. My bed was very modern and cream coloured with a spring frame of course, a brand new mattress and a feather mattress on top. I used a down padded spread as a bolster. I had to because the bedding was so soft that my pillow just sank into it. There was a white enamelled wash cabinet, another white enamelled glass topped locker, and a display unit with glass shelves, on which I kept my writing materials, books, etc. There was also a little round table with a red tablecloth, an armchair, a wall mirror. Just over my head in bed was a luxury reading lamp.

This hotel was in the village of Dassel and is 43 miles south of Hannover. It was a fairly large town and, of course, we were the only troops there. It was a place full of quaint old houses, built largely of wood.

Guard duties were frequent, but there were no fatigue duties. There were some Polish men who worked in the kitchens They were brought here as forced labour and, as they couldn't get back to their country, they did our work for food and cigarettes, etc. Eventually it was a case of getting Germans organised to do these duties for us.

On our way there we passed through Hannover and it was almost totally destroyed. It was difficult to find any building still standing. I remember seeing one building that looked intact but, as we passed it, I realised it was only a front wall, there was nothing behind it.

When we mounted guard duty it was very much a "spit and polish" occasion as we had to impress the local population.

One day I was on guard, when the Battery Sergeant Major and I were called to meet two old ladies at the entrance to our billet. The BSM asked me to translate their conversation. It was to the effect that a rather drunk Russian forced labour worker had been to their house which was isolated at the edge of the wood, and threatened them. They had two invalid husbands and they were afraid. We promised to send a patrol there a few times to make sure that they were alright. We did so and there was no further trouble.

There was now much speculation about our future. There was the possibility that we would be transferred to a different regiment and posted to another theatre of war. We didn't relish the thought and in fact nothing happened in that direction. It was now the 14th June 1945.

On the 17th or 18th June we were on the move again and, this time, to the town of Sarstedt. We were there for a particular dangerous task. An ammunition train had pulled into the station and caught fire. On it were 500 lb. bombs, landmines, etc., as well as artillery shells and small arms ammunition. There had been three major explosions and hundreds of smaller ones. In the centre of the railway track was a crater, similar to those made by 'ten ton tess' bombs. There were remains of wagons blown anywhere up to half a mile away. We made our quarters in a factory, again about half a mile from the site. In the factory yard was a ten foot length of railway line blown there by the explosions. Some houses nearer to the railway line were completely destroyed, probably with much loss of life. One oil tanker wagon had been blown off the track and was standing about a hundred yards away in an allotment. There were shells, mortar bombs, etc. scattered everywhere in the vicinity, the area was littered with them so we had to be very careful where we stepped. The first time that I had to walk along the track was in the middle of the night and I was very pleased when I reached the road again.

Just behind the factory was a transit camp for forced labour Russians, Poles, Yugoslavs, Latvians, etc. A Lance Bombardier and I had to patrol this camp as these men were leaving on their way to a transit camp somewhere, on their way home. We were conscious of the fact that they would destroy everything that they could as they left, including setting fire to the buildings, but we wanted to use the buildings ourselves. There was one Pole who was determined to run back from the group and start a fire. We had to fix our bayonets and chase him away.

Living in a small group in Sarstedt meant that we had very good food. We were able to buy eggs and other food from the local farms. Every morning the cooks would find a bucket of cherries, gooseberries, red currants and strawberries inside the cookhouse. We never knew where they came from and we didn't enquire ! The factory was called Voss Works and had in peacetime, made electric and gas cookers, etc. In wartime they had been making field kitchens, gun wheels, etc. A large amount of slave labour was used here and they were housed in a wooden huts. Some of these were still occupied by the slave labourers. The huts were surrounded by barbed wire fences with a guard's patrol space between each line of fence. The beds were double tier bunks packed so close that you could hardly get between them. There was only a very small area where the occupants could walk around. A notice said that they would be shot without warning if they acted suspiciously. One poor blighter had tried to make himself a comb out of a small piece of metal but, due to a lack of proper tools, the teeth were about a quarter of a inch across.

As an army of occupation it was our duty to remove from the area surrounding our base all traces of Nazism. A start was made by laying out a map and from it selecting at random a one kilometre grid square. We then visited that spot and recorded any signs of German military occupation

This could include anything from defence structures, weapons, ammunition, down to swastika signs or badges. I had a couple of soldiers detailed to help me in one such search.

One of these kilometre squares that I searched had within it a small school. The Headmistress lived in accommodation in or adjacent to the school grounds. I contacted this lady and asked her to open up the school premises so that I could inspect the classrooms, etc.. In what was probably the school hall, there were propaganda pictures of German battleships, submarines, personnel, etc., all displaying the swastika sign. I turned to the Headmistress and said something like "I cannot allow any Nazi pictures to remain here. They will have to come down and I will take them away with me." She tried to speak to me, but was terrified to the extent that she was quite unable to talk. It was almost as if she expected to be taken outside and shot. She would have seen, as was the policy, that we had our arms with us. I am sure that I did manage to calm her down before we left.

One day at the beginning of September, I went to the Divisional Sports and an Officer asked three of us surveyors to do all the measuring required, for the long jump, etc. The announcer, when he wanted us, always asked for the three gunner surveyors. Once he saw me and noticed my stripes, he grinned and said "I get annoyed at being demoted", joking of course. So he announced over the loudhailers "There is one more alteration," this time not to the programme. One of the surveyors is a Bombardier, so it's "The Bombardier and two Gunners".

In Sarstedt we had a Hotel complete with staff that became our equivalent of a NAFFI. It was of quite a high standard and had a very attractive set of waitresses. One was a rather dark haired girl and we called her 'the gypsy'. One day she served me and I commented on the very attractive china on which my snack was served. I said that "I wish I could buy some crockery like that." "The gypsy" walked away and then ran out of the hotel. I asked another waitress what the matter was and she said that she had felt insulted when I commented on the tip I had given her. She had obviously misunderstood what I had said about the cost of something. I ran out of the building to try and find her and put things right. She was leaning on the railings on the side of a footbridge over the road, sobbing away. Fortunately I was able to talk to her and convince her that she had misunderstood my words. Another international dispute settled !!

In the middle of October 1945 the situation was that Germany was divided into four zones, Soviet Russian, British, American and French, the latter three being known as the 'Western Zones'. Berlin itself was divided into four 'Sectors', all deep within the Soviet Russian zone. In order to get supplies of food, medicines, coal, etc. to the Western Sectors of the city, the supply routes had to cross Soviet held territory. It was in connection with this latter that I got involved.

I was instructed to take a small number of troops to form a guard on one of these coal trains. We were given supplies for the journey and full instructions as to our rights, details of our destination and what to do after we had safely delivered the train to its unloading point (Plate 18).

We picked up this coal laden train of many trucks. There were a couple of Royal Engineers on the train but their role was simply to control the engine driver and his assistant. I was responsible for the safe delivery of the coal and all negotiations on the journey. The journey to Berlin was completely uneventful. It was a very slow progress and many stops on the way, but eventually we got there. We had a couple of days in Berlin before we would have to return with an empty train of trucks.

At five o'clock it was announced over the loudhailer that all the train guards, with the exception of those under the command of Bdr. Cole and Bdr. Forbes could leave camp. The two Bdrs. were to report to the office for moving off instructions. This we did and found that we were to be transported to Berlin Grunewald station. It meant that we had only about one hour to get packed and ready for the off. In the rush to get sorted we landed up with twice the amount of rations that we really should have had. (We also had quite a lot saved from our outward journey as well). We reached Grunewald at about seven o'clock in the evening and moved into static railway coaches fitted out as bedrooms, and there was also a cookhouse and a dining hall, all converted from railway coaches.

It was clear that Bdr. Forbes would be moving off about midnight, I wouldn't be off until the following mid-morning. One of my guards was wandering along the platform and was approached by two young women who were waiting complete with their rucksacks and, in common with hundreds of others, were hoping to be able to get to the British Sector, but they did not have the necessary papers to permit them to do so. We decided that these were very decent girls, probably nurses, and decided to help them. One of the girls had a friend so we said she could travel as well. Whilst we were out patrolling the platform we said that they could get into our coach and get some sleep. When we got back into our coach, we played cards to keep ourselves awake, just in case we were called out for anything. At half past three we decided we just had to get some sleep ourselves, so, as the girls were in our beds, we bedded down on the floor.

The civilian guard who had travelled to Berlin with our train, liked our group so managed to get allocated to us for the return journey.

At one o'clock we were ready to move off. The two Royal Engineers decided that they would chose which coach they travelled in, and which we could have. They didn't know who they were dealing with, so were told in no uncertain terms that their job was the engine cab, and that I was in charge of the train and told them which carriage they could have. (Fancy challenging Bdr. Cole - no contest!)

Our first halt was at another Berlin station which was absolutely crowded with people wanting to travel in our direction. They immediately started to get into the wagons, so I sent the guard down to turf them off. As a result the people were almost fighting to get to me to show me the papers they had . But only one had the necessary Russian permit (Incidentally she had lived in Torquay at some time or other).

The pleading went on, sometimes in German and sometimes in English. One old lady was catching hold of my blouse, pleading in German for a lift, but it was no use, I couldn't say "yes" to only one of them. After a short time it was obviously impossible for three men to keep three or four thousand people out of our 67 trucks, so I said that people could travel to Magdeburg, but there the Russians would order them off the train. In just a few moments it was being announced over the station loudspeakers, so the rush was on, and they would be in open trucks for some 15 hours, all through the night.

A Polish man came to me with his wife and said "Some Russians have come into my truck and I am feared for my wife. You know that the Russians are continually raping German and other women. Will one of you English soldiers please sleep with my wife and then she will be alright." Just imagine it, a man asking a stranger, but a stranger that he trusts, if his wife can sleep with him, because he knows she would not be brutally treated.

A Russian soldier who was a bit tipsy, went to the coach next to ours which the R.Es were using and in an attempt to get in, produced a revolver. The men who had tried to bully me, lost their bluster and asked me, to deal with him. He didn't fancy his chances when I got my soldiers to fix their bayonets.

After another short journey, we stopped again and someone brought a little girl, about twelve years old, to ask if she could travel with us. They said her parents had been shot by the Russians and she was wanting to get to relations in the British Zone.

Two of the young women we had said could travel with us volunteered to act as cooks. We were glad of all those extra rations that had come our way. To save time, whenever we could we made our tea with boiling water from the engine.

As we approached Magdeburg, we told the girls that they would have to get into our beds and pretend they were troops sleeping. At Magdeburg eleven Russians piled into our coach. I asked if anyone spoke English. No-one did so it was "Spricht man Deutsch hier?" This time the officer said "Ja." I told him, in German, that we were the English train guard. He explained to the others and they got off our coach.

From Magdeburg we moved on to Marienberg, and then it was about six or seven kilometres to the Zone Control point. At the control it was obvious that the Russians had a large number of soldiers ready to search our train. I stood in the doorway of our coach, cleaning my nails and looking innocent.

The girls were wearing our spare blouses but, of course it didn't fool the Russian Officer. He came in and said "Any civilians", saying "No" was no good, because he was having a good look around. He said "O.K." and one of my men gave him some cigarettes and I gave him a tin of bully beef. He went off a pleased man.

The train started off and was gathering speed when the Russians gave a Belgian and his wife permission to cross into our Zone. They started to run for it and the wife had just got her hands on to the floor of our coach as she collapsed. Luckily a few seconds previously we had grabbed hold of her arms and so were able to haul her aboard. The husband got on alright. By the time we got to Helmstedt she was a lot better. We learnt from the man that she was pregnant. We got her safely to a Red Cross station for treatment.

My first job on arrival was to hand in my consignment note to say that I had brought the train back complete. I went back to our coach and my chaps said that a Bdr. had been and said that we had to get our kit out on to a nearby road, where a truck would take us to a transit camp. I went and saw this fellow and told him that we were not going to lug our kit over about twenty railway lines and then only land up in a transit camp. I went along to the German railway man in charge of these sidings, and told him that our truck had to be taken to Hanover Someone else came and said if we didn't get ourselves out, we would land up in some sidings about five miles away. I said "That's alright we've got some sleep to make up."

We got the girls to leave the train and go up to an adjacent road where they could try to get further help.

From a nearby signal box I rang up the sidings railway train operator, told him where we were, and where we needed to get to. In next to no time an engine came up just for our one coach. We were taken down into the station's sidings where we had about a two hour wait, until being coupled up to a civilian train going to Sarstedt.

The young girl who had teamed up with me was called Gerda. She lived in Cuxhaven, and gave me her address and said that if I travelled back through that port, to make myself known to her parents. She was an extremely nice person. She was married to a sailor in the German Navy and she didn't know if he was alive or dead.

On the 31st October 1945 I was out with a patrol all night, trying to ambush an armed raiding party that was operating in the area, a rather scary operation. We did not make contact with them, but tried for several days afterwards without success. In doing this we got into all sorts of positions and often came back, caked in mud and looking like a band of pirates. I wore a woollen cap, a padded short jacket with a hood, two pairs of trousers and two pairs of socks. In the interests of keeping warm, we disregarded appearance and did look really scruffy. We were bristling with arms to support that pirate look. I always went out with my rifle and bayonet, hand grenades stuffed in my pockets and a lovely little dagger for close combat. The dagger was a German Commando dagger and was as sharp as a razor. Would you have liked to meet me on a dark night? At that time the temperature was about four degrees below zero, and there was plenty of snow about.

In Sarstedt Sgt. Wally Wicks acted as the equivalent of Town Clerk, as the senior resident British soldier. My role, being an aggressive type, was to do all the arresting. I should add that Wally worked, in civilian life, in the fraud department of the National Savings Bank. He could speak German, French, Italian, Spanish, Russian, Serbo-Croat, and he actually left the regiment

П Р О П У С К.

ПРЕДЪЯВИТЕЛЬ СЕГО НАЗНАЧЕН СТАРШИМ ВОЕННОЙ ОХРАНЫ ПОЕЗДА, КОТОРЫЙ ВОЗИТ УГОЛЬ ИЗ БРИТАНСКОГО РАЙОНА В БЕРЛИН.

ВО ВСЕХ СЛУЧАЯХ ПРЕДЪЯВЛЕНИЯ ПРОПУСКА ЛИЦАМ ВОЕННЫМ ПРЕДСТАВИТЕЛЯМ ИЛИ КОНТРОЛЬНЫМ ОРГАНАМ СОВЕТСКОЙ АРМИИ КОМАНДОВАНИЕ ПЯТОЙ ДИВИЗИИ БРИТАНСКОЙ АРМИИ ПРОСИТ ОКАЗЫВАТЬ ВСЯКОЕ СОДЕЙСТВИЕ В БЫСТРЕЙШЕЙ ДОСТАВКЕ ЭШЕЛОНА В БРИТАНСКУЮ ЗОНУ г.БЕРЛИН.

Командир 5 с.д.Британской Армии
Полковник

PASS.

THE BEARER OF THIS PASS HAS BEEN DETAILED AS NCO IC COAL TRAIN GUARD PROCEEDING TO THE BERLIN AREA AND SUBSEQUENTLY RETURNING TO THE BRITISH ZONE.

SOVIET AUTHORITIES TO WHOM THIS PASS MAY BE PRESENTED ARE REQUESTED TO ASSIST THE GUARD IN CARRYING OUT HIS DUTIES.

GS
5 Brit Inf Div

▲ Plate 18

eventually to study Japanese and Chinese at the School of Oriental Languages somewhere in Cornwall.

On the morning of the 10th December 1945 I had to take a party to arrest three people wanted by the Field Security Unit. The first one had been living in Czechoslovakia for the past two years, the next was a prisoner in American hands and the third was working at the local gas works. When we got there, he was missing, because he had gone to the bank, so we instructed the two civilian policemen who were with us to find him and bring him back to our camp. Later on I took two guards with me to collect him. We took him to his home to collect washing kit, etc and then whip him off to the Security Section. As soon as we got to his home, his wife and daughter flung their arms around his neck, crying their eyes out. There were also two old ladies crying but not making such a to-do. The daughter would break away, say something and then start howling again, flinging her arms around him and calling us swine. Of course, I could have arrested her on the spot for contempt of British soldiers, but under the circumstances, although I was a temporary interpreter, I pretended not to understand what she was saying.

I was out and about, on and off, arresting people. It usually was a case of having someone come to us and denounce a person as having been in the SS. I think it was often more a case of trying to take revenge on someone, rather than the person actually having been in the SS. I remember taking three men to the prison in Hildersheim. One started to move his position, so I made them stand to attention all the time they were waiting to be taken over by the Prison Governor. He said to me that he didn't believe that these men were ex SS men, but they had to go in for interrogation.

A step forward to 13th January 1946. My address is no longer "A" Troop, "B" Battery, 9th Survey Regiment R.A., but now it is "E" Troop, 58 Battery, 25th Field Regiment R.A. The Technical regiment were disbanded as there was no role for us when the fighting ended. We became simply an Army of Occupation.

I wrote home a letter as follows: "Guess what ! I've got a gun and when I say a 'gun' I mean a gun, not just a rifle. It's a 25 pounder complete with two ammunition limbers. When I first saw it I thought it was brand new but it is actually far from it. All the brasswork and bright steel is kept highly polished with metal polish so you can guess what it looks like. But wait a minute, this isn't all I've been given by far. In addition I have a jeep, a half tracked armoured car, and a Quad (the vehicles used for towing guns). In addition to all these material things, I've got a gun crew of about fourteen men. So you can see the things I shall be getting up to for a while to come.

Another thing about our life here. Rank in these Field Regiments is considered far more than in the old regiment. Just a couple of examples. We are not allowed to sleep in rooms where lower ranks sleep and we have a Mess of our own and daren't show foot inside the Gunners' Canteen. Sounds a bit snootiest I know but remember there is a completely different type of fellow here to the 9th and need a more disciplined life to keep them in order."

We had a smashing club in the town, run by my new Regiment. It was complete with games rooms, library, lounge, dining lounge, reading and writing rooms, in all a very nice place. From the window of my billet I could see the famous Hertz Mountains where winter sports are held. (We had 175 pairs of skis in the Regiment!) We were close to Bad Hertzburg the famous winter resort.

I had to remove the 1st Corps Spearhead badge from my uniform and replace it with the "Y" badge of my new Division.

I was only in this new Regiment for a few weeks when I had a call to the Office. I was told that my English employers had requested my release from Service on what was known as a Class "B" release.

British employers could request the return of their former employees to work on important work back in our own country. I couldn't sign the papers quick enough.

After getting all my equipment together, I was taken to the railway station to start my journey home. Into the carriage, where I was seated, came a young soldier who explained that he was a dental technician. He had been sent from England, but when he arrived at his unit in Germany, they were not ready to receive him so he was sent back on leave to await another posting. He fell asleep and, at one point on the journey, when the train stopped, he woke up and said "What station is this ? Oh, I can see what it is, it's HERREN," and went back to sleep. What he had seen was the name board showing the location of the gent's toilet. Back home he would have said that he travelled through Germany and stopped at Herren. They wouldn't have found it on any map !!

In a very short time I was back in England, in Woolwich Arsenal, where I was fitted out with my "demob." clothes and given my train warrant to get home to Paignton.

My previous employers, Vanstone & Sons, had a major contract to develop a large prefab housing estate in Hele Village, Torquay. They had a retired Army Major in charge of the site but, as an engineer, he had an appointment to become the Engineer to an African State Railway. Vanstones had no-one who could take his place and considered that, with my added years in the army,

I could do the job.

I spent several weeks working under the Major, and learning from him all the time. When he left, the Ministry of Works accepted me as the site Agent, in charge of the site at Hele.

So ended my wartime exploits.

Statistics

Statistics, published at the end of the war, record that although the 9th Survey Regiment R.A. was, by army standards, a very small unit (just over 2000 personnel, of which 469 were flash spotters) we suffered a total of eight 'killed in action' and sixty seven 'wounded in action'.

The 9th Survey Regiment R.A. was awarded the following Decorations and Mentions for Gallantry :-

Order of the British Empire - once

George Medal - once

Member of the British Empire - four times

Military Cross - once

Military Medal - twice

Chevalier of the Order of Leopold II with palm (Belgium) - twice

Croix de Guerre 1940 (Belgium) - seven times

Croix de Guerre (France) - twice

Mentioned in Dispatches - seven times

Commander-in-Chief's Certificate - five times.

Appendices

Extract from General Sir Brian Horrocks's (Jorrocks')
book "CORPS COMMANDER".

Since the war I have often paid tribute to the part
that our Royal Artillery played. The core of the Royal
Artillery was the fantastic accuracy of their Survey Units.
The one I knew best was a pre-war Territorial Unit, 4th
(Durham) Survey Regiment from Gateshead. I first met them
in the Middle East and we were then together until the end
of the war and I came to rely on them completely ...
(page 177)

Paragraph describing the Battle for the lower Rhine
Bridgehead :-

The German gunners who had survived the first
bombardment now rushed to man and fire their guns. The
positions of these batteries had previously been
accurately surveyed by our flash spotters and sound
rangers of the Survey Regiment. Then after ten minutes, the
original barrage started again, concentrating particularly
on the German guns which had been located. In addition
to the artillery, each division also what we called the 'pepper
the 'pepper pot'. Every weapon not actually in the
assault opened up on the German positions. The effect was
so devastating that, when the attack really went in later on,
the German gunners remained crouched in their trenches.
(pages 184/5)

▲ Plate 19

90

It's the
BEST
NEWS
we have had for
a long time

So say Mum & Dad

WE'RE SO GLAD YOU'RE COMING HOME

As each country was liberated from German occupation, there was a great sense of euphoria. This resulted in much cheering of the troops as they passed through crowds of people, giving hugs and kisses, as well as gifts of fruit etc.

Very quickly celebrating postcards were produced, with patriotic symbols and another type which were aimed at ridiculing the Germans.

The following pages give examples of both kinds.

POUR LES ALLIÉS,
REMPLI D'AMOUR,
MON P'TIT CŒUR BAT COMME U[...]

LEVE DE GEALLIEERDEN
MAAR LEVE OOK MIJN JASS.

DE ZEELANDSCHE,
  GE ZIET HET KLAAR,
ONTVANGT DE GEALLIEERDEN
  MET MILD GEBAAR.

Propaganda leaflets

During the Second World War, propaganda leaflets were dropped from planes on to troops below. These were thrown from an aircraft and the slipstream scattered them over quite a large area.

There is one example I encountered that was dropped on British soldiers, and the content shows that it must have been in the early days of the Normandy invasion.

The leaflets in German were dropped by our own forces on to the German positions, encouraging them to become prisoners of war, rather than be in an army facing destruction.

Wer wird Deutschland wieder aufbauen?

Who Will Reconstruct Germany?

(Front, see page 100 for reverse)

Hier fängt der Wiederaufbau an

Aus dem Kanada-Lager Nr. 133
— einem von vielen:

9 Klassen mit durchschnittlich 45 Mann Belegschaft bereiten auf die höhere und mittlere Beamtenlaufbahn vor, mit anschliessender Abschlussprüfung.
In der Lager-Universität finden Vorlesungen in folgenden Fächern statt : Recht, Medizin, Philologie, Naturwissenschaften und Technik. Durchschnittliche Zahl der Vorlesungsstunden pro Woche in jedem Fach 15 bis 20, in Medizin 30. Die Anerkennung der von der Lager-Universität erteilten Prüfungsdiplome durch die deutschen Hochschulen steht bevor. Ferner ist ein landwirtschaftlicher Kurs vorhanden, der auf die Laufbahn des Diplom-Landwirts vorbereitet.
Weitere Unterrichtskurse : Sprachen (Englisch, Französisch, Spanisch, Russisch), Technik (Maschinenbau, allgemeine Technik, Elektrotechnik), Handwerk. Die Lager-bibliothek umfasst 20.000 Bände. Ausserdem stehen 7000 wissenschaftliche Werke zur Verfügung.

Sie werden Deutschland wieder aufbauen!

The Reconstruction Starts Here

From Canada Camp No. 133 - one of many:

9 classes with an average of 45 men prepare for higher and middle career paths in the civil service, including a final examination.

The following lectures take place in the camp university: law, medicine, philology, science and technology. Average hours of lectures per week in each subject of 15 to 20, 30 in medicine. Recognition for the camp university's diplomas from the German colleges is imminent. In addition an agriculture course is planned, that will prepare students for a diploma in agriculture.

Other courses: languages (English, French, Spanish, Russian), technology (engineering, general technology, electronics), handicraft. The camp library contains 20,000 volumes. Additionally, 7000 academic works are available.

They will rebuild Germany!

Hier fängt der Wiederaufbau an

Aus einem amerikanischen Gefangenenlager — einem von vielen:

9 Klassen mit durchschnittlich 45 Mann Belegschaft bereiten die Teilnehmer auf die höhere und mittlere Beamtenlaufbahn vor, mit anschliessender Abschlussprüfung.

In der Lager-Universität finden Vorlesungen in folgenden Fächern statt: Recht, Medizin, Philologie, Naturwissenschaften und Technik. Durchschnittliche Zahl der Vorlesungsstunden pro Woche in jedem Fach 15 bis 20, in Medizin 30. Die Anerkennung der von der Lager-Universität erteilten Prüfungsdiplome durch die deutschen Hochschulen steht bevor. Ferner ist ein landwirtschaftlicher Kurs vorhanden, der auf die Laufbahn des Diplom-Landwirts vorbereitet.

Weitere Unterrichtskurse: Sprachen (Englisch, Französisch, Spanisch, Russisch), Technik (Maschinenbau, allgemeine Technik, Elektrotechnik), Handwerk. Die Lagerbibliothek umfasst tausende von Bänden. Ausserdem stehen zahlreiche wissenschaftliche Werke zur Verfügung.

Sie werden Deutschland wieder aufbauen!

Z.G. 74.

The Reconstruction Starts Here

From an American prison camp -
one of many:

9 classes with an average of 45 men prepare for higher and middle career paths in the civil service, including a final examination.

The following lectures take place in the camp university: law, medicine, philology, science and technology. Average hours of lectures per week in each subject of 15 to 20, 30 in medicine. Recognition for the camp university's diplomas from the German colleges is imminent. In addition an agriculture course is planned, that will prepare students for a diploma in agriculture.

Other courses: languages (English, French, Spanish, Russian), technology (engineering, general technology, electronics), handicraft. The camp library consists of thousands of volumes.

Additionally, umpteen academic works are available.

They will rebuild Germany

(Front, see page 104 for reverse)

SOLDATENPFLICHT

Fünf Jahre lang hat der deutsche Soldat an allen Fronten seine Pflicht erfüllt. Dabei hat er die schwersten Opfer gebracht.

Die vielen Siege früherer Jahre haben ihm jedoch auf die Dauer nichts genützt.

Heute rücken die Russen von Osten immer näher heran. Rom ist gefallen und die neue Schlacht von Frankreich ist im Gang.

Auf allen Seiten bringt sich die Übermacht der Gegner zur Geltung. Deutschland kann heute nicht mehr hoffen, den Krieg zu gewinnen. Es kann ihn nur noch verlängern.

Eure Soldatenpflicht ist getan

Eine andere Pflicht bleibt jedoch übrig:

Die Pflicht zur Selbsterhaltung

Eure Familie, Euer Volk und Euer Vaterland brauchen gesunde Helfer zum Wiederaufbau, nicht weitere unnütze Opfer für eine verlorene Sache.

Als Soldaten ist Euch gute Behandlung im Fall der Gefangenschaft nach den Bestimmungen der Genfer Konvention durch die Alliierten verbürgt.

A Soldier's Duty

For five years the German soldier has fulfilled his duty on all fronts. In doing so he has made the hardest sacrifices.

The many victories of former years have not helped him in the long term, however.

Today the Russians approach ever nearer from the East. Rome has fallen and the new French campaign is in progress.

On all sides the stronger might of the opposition is being asserted. Germany can no longer hope to win the war. It can only prolong it.

Your soldier's duty has been done. Another duty remains however: The duty of self-preservation.

Your family, your people and your fatherland need healthy helpers for reconstruction, not more wasted victims of a lost cause.

As soldiers you are guaranteed good treatment by the Allies if you are captured according to the Geneva Convention.

SIE FEHLT...

Frage einen alten Frontsoldaten, der den Frankreich-Feldzug 1940 oder den Afrika-Feldzug 1941 mitgemacht hat, was ihm heute am meisten fehlt. Die erste Antwort, die er dir geben wird, ist : Am meisten fehlt uns die Luftwaffe !

● **für Aufklärung:** Damals konnten die Fieseler Storchs und Arados noch ungestört aufklären, während der Feind im Dunkeln blieb. Resultat : Überraschungsangriffe und Durchbrüche. Heute ist die Lage umgekehrt.

● **für Nachschub:** Damals rollte der deutsche Nachschub unbehindert zur Front, während Stukas und Jabos dem Feind die Nachschubstrassen zerschlugen. Heute ist der deutsche Nachschub unterbunden, die Lage umgekehrt.

● **für Fronteinsatz:** Die grossen deutschen Durchbrüche 1940 und 1941 erfolgten mit rollendem Stuka-Einsatz. Heute sind es die Mitchells, Marauders, Typhoons und Spitfires, die den Weg für Durchbrüche bereiten.

Frage einen alten Frontsoldaten, was in einer hoffnungslosen Lage zu tun ist, wenn der Einsatz des Lebens dem Vaterland nicht mehr nützen kann. Er wird dir sagen : Wenn es nicht anders geht, dann lässt man sich eben gefangennehmen !

106

It's lacking ...

Ask an old soldier of the front, who took part in the French campaign in 1940 or the Africa campaign in 1941, what he is lacking most today. The first answer that he will give is: we miss the air force most of all!

● for intelligence: back then the Fieseler, Storchs and Arados could still reconnoitre unopposed, whilst the enemy was in the dark. The result: surprise attacks and advances. Today the situation is the other way around.

● or supplies: back then German supplies arrived unhindered at the front, whilst Stukas and Jabos destroyed the enemy's supply routes. Today German supplies have been cut off, the situation is the other way around.

● for deployment at the front: the big German advances of 1940 and 1941 resulted from continuous Stuka deployment. Today it is the Mitchells, Marauders, Typhoons and Spitfires that prepare the way for advancement.

Ask an old soldier of the front, what can be done in a hopeless situation, if the deployment of men can no longer help the Fatherland. He will tell you: if there is no other option, then let yourself be taken into custody!

(Front, see page 108 for reverse)

DAS RÄTSEL
der deutschen Luftwaffe

(Lösung siehe unten)

IM OSTEN

wird euren Kameraden erklärt, die Luftwaffe werde für die Abwehrkämpfe im Westen benötigt. Hier im Westen wurde den Kameraden der 91. I.D. erzählt, die Luftwaffe decke den Rückzug in Polen und Ostpreussen. *Wie erklärt sich das?*

IM SÜDEN

wird euren Kameraden gesagt, die Luftwaffe sei bei Cherbourg zusammengezogen worden. In Cherbourg warteten 50 000 Kameraden vergeblich auf Luftunterstützung. Die 243. I.D. bekam in 15 Tagen 1 deutsches Flugzeug zu sehen. *Wie erklärt sich das?*

IM WESTEN

wird noch immer mit dem Verbleib der Luftwaffe Schindluder getrieben, indem man den Verteidigern von St. Lô sagte, die Luftwaffe müsse in die Panzerschlachten bei Caen eingreifen. In Caen war sie aber auch nicht. *Wie erklärt sich das?*

DES RÄTSELS LÖSUNG: Die Luftwaffe existiert. Sie ist zu Hause, im Westen und im Süden. Aber sie reicht nirgends aus. Genau wie die englisch-französische Luftwaffe im Frankreich-Feldzug 1940, kann sie infolge ihrer Unterlegenheit oft nicht starten und erleidet schon auf den Flugfeldern schwere Verluste. Und da sie die Flugzeugfabriken nicht mehr verteidigen kann, ist auch der Ersatz nicht mehr zureichend. So wird sie eben dauernd kleiner.

ZG 36 A

108

The Riddle of the German Air Force

Answers below

In the East
Your comrades have been told the air force is needed for the defence battles in the West. Here in the West the soldiers of the 91st Infantry are told that the air force is protecting the retreat in Poland and East Prussia. How do you explain that?

In the South
Your comrades have been told the air force has been assembled near Cherbourg. In Cherbourg 50,000 soldiers waited in vain for air support. The 243rd Infantry saw only 1 German plane in 15 days. How do you explain that?

In the West
There is still deception regarding the whereabouts of the air force, as the defenders of St. Lô were told that the air force had to engage in the tank battles near Caen. But they were not in Caen. How do you explain that?

The solution: the air force exists. It is at home, in the East, in the West and in the South, but it cannot help. Just like the English and French air forces in the French campaign in 1940, it cannot take off because of its inferiority and it even suffers massive damages on the airfields. And, as they cannot defend the aeroplane factories anymore, replacements are not sufficient anymore either. Therefore its size is ever shrinking.

RÜCKZUG ?
Nein — schlimmer !

Der gesamte linke Flügel der Westfront befindet sich in Auflösung. Amerikanische Panzereinheiten haben die ganze Bretagne durchquert, Brest im Westen und den Loire-Fluss im Süden erreicht. Weitere schwere motorisierte und Panzer-Kolonnen stossen nach Osten vor und drohen, die gesamte Front aufzurollen. Damit beginnt nicht nur der unvermeidliche deutsche Rückzug. Damit beginnt der unvermeidliche Zusammenbruch im Westen.

Die Ursachen sind jedem erfahrenen Soldaten klar :

- *Panzer- und Luftüberlegenheit der Alliierten wirken sich erst jetzt voll aus.*
- *Ohne Luftdeckung bedeutet jede Bewegung bei Tag ein ungeheuerliches Gemetzel.*
- *Von Frontverkürzung ist keine Rede. Die Front wird von jetzt an immer länger.*
- *Damit ist den Alliierten Gelegenheit gegeben, immer mehr Material einzusetzen.*
- *Für einen raschen Rückzug fehlt es an Fahrzeugen, Treibstoff und Eisenbahnen.*

Das sind Tatsachen, die von Dir eine klare, dringende Entscheidung fordern : Entweder Du entscheidest Dich, das blutige Spiessrutenlaufen mitzumachen ; oder Du beschliesst, Dein Leben für die Heimat zu erhalten. Viele werden gänzlich nutzlos sterben müssen — knapp vor Kriegsende. Es gibt für Dich nur eine Rettung : Zurückbleiben und Dich gefangennehmen lassen.

Die Entscheidung drängt !

ZG.44

Retreat?

No - worse!

The entire left flank of the western front is breaking up. American tank units have passed through the whole of Brittany and reached Brest in the west and the Loire River in the south. Further mobile tank units are pushing to the east and threaten to push back the entire front. So begins not only the unavoidable German retreat, but also the unavoidable collapse in the West.

● The reasons are clear to every experienced soldier:

● The tank and air superiority of the Allies is only just starting to have a massive effect

● The lack of air support means that every movement in the day results in an enormous massacre

● There is no talk of a shortening of the front. The front from now on will get ever longer

● Therefore the Allies have the chance to use ever more equipment

● Motor vehicles, fuel and trains are lacking for a quick retreat

These are facts that demand a clear and urgent response from you: either you decide to run the bloody gauntlet; or you resolve to save your life for home. Many will have to die entirely unnecessarily - shortly before the end of the war. There is only one rescue for you: Stay behind and let yourself be taken into custody.

A decision is needed!

(Front, see page 112 for reverse)

SOLDATENPFLICHT

Fünf Jahre lang hat der deutsche Soldat an allen Fronten seine Pflicht erfüllt. Dabei hat er die schwersten Opfer gebracht. Die vielen Siege früherer Jahre haben ihm jedoch auf die Dauer nichts genützt.

Heute stehen die Russen auf deutschem Reichsgebiet in Ostpreussen. Sie haben Lemberg genommen, die Weichsel überquert und stehen vor Warschau. In Frankreich sind die Alliierten durchgebrochen und werfen immer neues Material in den Einsatz.

Angesichts der Übermacht auf allen Seiten kann Deutschland nicht mehr hoffen, den Krieg zu gewinnen. Es kann ihn nur noch verlängern.

Eure Soldatenpflicht ist getan

Eine andere Pflicht bleibt jedoch übrig:

Die Pflicht zur Selbsterhaltung

Eure Familie, Euer Volk und Euer Vaterland brauchen gesunde Helfer zum Wiederaufbau, nicht weitere unnütze Opfer für eine verlorene Sache.

Als Soldaten ist Euch gute Behandlung im Fall der Gefangenschaft nach den Bestimmungen der Genfer Konvention durch die Alliierten verbürgt.

A Soldier's Duty

For five years the German soldier has fulfilled his duty on all fronts. In doing so he has made the hardest sacrifices. The many victories of former years have not helped him in the long term however.

Today the Russians are in the German Reich's territory in East Prussia. They have taken Lviv (then Lemberg), crossed the Vistula and stand before Warsaw. In France the Allies are advancing and constantly throwing new equipment into deployment.

Given the superiority on all sides, Germany can no longer hope to win the war. It can only prolong it.

Your soldier's duty has been done

Another duty remains however:

The duty of self-preservation

Your family, your people and your fatherland need healthy helpers for reconstruction, not more wasted victims of a lost cause.

As soldiers, if you are captured, you are guaranteed good treatment by the Allies according to the Geneva Convention.

Im Osten

kapituliert Generalleutnant Müller, als seine 4. Armee im Raum von Minsk durch den überraschenden russischen Vormarsch abgeschnitten wird. Am 8. Juli 1944 erlässt er folgenden Befehl an seine Truppen östlich von Minsk:

Soldaten der 4. Armee!

Nach einer Woche schwerer Kämpfe und Märsche ist unsere Lage hoffnungslos geworden. Wir haben unsere Pflicht erfüllt. Unsere Kampfkraft ist auf ein Minimum gesunken, und es besteht keinerlei Hoffnung auf Nachschub. Laut Mitteilung des OKW stehen die Russen bei der Stadt Baranovitschi. Die letzten Linien über den nächsten Wasserlauf sind uns abgeschnitten. Es besteht keinerlei Hoffnung, mit unseren Kräften und Mitteln von hier zu entkommen. Unsere Verbände sind regellos zerstreut. Eine riesige Anzahl von Verwundeten musste ohne jede Hilfe im Stich gelassen werden.

Das russische Oberkommando hat versprochen: a) ärztliche Hilfe für die Verwundeten; b) den Offizieren den Degen, den Soldaten die Orden zu belassen.

Uns wurde vorgeschlagen, alle Waffen und Ausrüstung zu sammeln und unbeschädigt abzuliefern; den nutzlosen Widerstand einzustellen.

Ich befehle, den Kampf unverzüglich einzustellen. Die örtlichen Gruppen von 100 bis 500 Mann sammeln sich unter Führung der Offiziere oder rangältesten Unteroffiziere. Die Verwundeten werden gesammelt und mitgenommen. Wir müssen Disziplin und Haltung zeigen und mit der Ausführung dieser Massnahme möglichst schnell beginnen.

Dieser Befehl ist schriftlich, mündlich und mit allen Mitteln weiterzugeben.

MÜLLER, GENERALLEUTNANT
Kommandierender General des 12. Armeekorps.

In the East

Lieutenant General Müller surrenders as his 4th Army in the area of Minsk gets cut off by the surprise Russian advance. On the 8th July 1944 he issued the following recommendation to his troops east of Minsk:

Soldiers of the 4th Army!

After a week of hard fighting and marching our position has become hopeless. We have fulfilled our duty. Our fighting strength has dropped to a minimum and there is no hope of supplies. According to a message from the army's high command the Russians are situated near the town of Baranovitschi. The last routes across the nearest river have been cut off. No hope remains, with our strength and means, to escape from here. Our formations have been irregularly scattered. A great number of wounded have had to be abandoned without any aid.

The Russian High Command has promised:

a) medical help for the wounded;
b) to allow the officers of the sword control of their soldiers.

We have been advised to collect and deliver undamaged all weapons and equipment and the cessation of futile resistance.

I recommend that the fight is immediately stopped. The local groups of 100 to 500 men assemble under the command of the officer or the highest-ranked Sergeant. The wounded will be picked up and taken away. We must show discipline and poise and begin as quickly as possible with the execution of these measures.

This recommendation should be passed on in writing, verbally and in any other possible manner.

Müller, Lieutenant General

Commanding General of the 12th Army Corps

(Front, see page 116 for reverse)

Kein Vergnügen

Nein, Kriegsgefangenschaft ist kein Vergnügen. Kaum einer der 150 000 deiner Kameraden, die in amerikanischen Lagern sind, hat sich ergeben, weil er besonders gerne nach Amerika wollte. Sie mussten sich aber ergeben. Und immer häufiger geschieht es Kameraden, dass sie sich entscheiden müssen, ob sie die Heimat wiedersehen wollen — oder sterben. Und sie entscheiden sich :

Lieber frei als Kriegsgefangener
Lieber Kriegsgefangener als tot

Es mag kein Vergnügen sein, Kriegsgefangener zu werden, aber auf diese Tatsachen kannst du mit Bestimmtheit rechnen :

1 Du wirst als Soldat behandelt —

ohne Schikane, fair, wie es einem tapferen Gegner gebührt. In den Lagern herrscht, wo immer möglich, Selbstverwaltung. Das bedeutet: Deine eigenen Kameraden sind deine unmittelbaren Vorgesetzten.

2 Anständige Verpflegung

Gemäss der Genfer Konvention erhalten Kriegsgefangene dieselben Rationen wie Soldaten im amerikanischen Heer — dem bestgenährten Heer der Welt. Die Kost wird von Kameraden auf deutsche Weise zubereitet.

3 Lehr - und Sportbetrieb

In deiner Freizeit kannst du Sport betreiben oder dich an einem der vielen Bildungs- und Fachkurse beteiligen, die von Kameraden in den Lagern abgehalten werden. Du kannst dich für den Frieden vorbereiten.

4 Briefverkehr

Du kannst nach Hause schreiben — 4 Briefe und 4 Karten im Monat. Du kannst Briefe und auch Pakete erhalten. Aber was das Wichtigste ist : Du weisst mit Bestimmtheit, dass du die Heimat nach Kriegsende wiedersiehst.

Z.G 41A.

No Fun

No, war captivity is no fun. None of the 150,000 of your comrades that are in the American camps gave themselves up because they really wanted to go to America. They had to give themselves up. More and more comrades must decide, whether they want to see their homes again, or die. And they decide:

Better to be free than a prisoner of war
Better to be a prisoner of war than dead

It may not be fun to be a prisoner of war, but these facts you can surely understand:

1 **You will be treated as a soldier**
   without harassment, fair, like a valiant foe is due. In the camps individual responsibility, where possible, prevails. That means: your own comrades are your direct supervisors.

2 **Fair treatment**
   According to the Geneva Convention prisoners of war receive the same rations as soldiers in the American army - the best fed army in the world. The food is prepared by comrades according to German methods.

3 **Lectures and physical activity**
   In your free time you can play sports or take part in one of the many specialist courses that are run by comrades in the camp. You can prepare for freedom.

4 **Correspondence**
   You can write home - 4 letters and 4 cards a month. You can receive letters and also parcels. But the most important is: youknow that will see your home .

Calling

S. O. S.

GERMANS

SEND US

DOCTORS !

That's the
CRY
of the
1ˢᵗ American Army
near St Lô.

Who knows, perhaps

you

**may be in the same desperate
situation to-morrow.**

AW 41.

Letters to parents
whilst on active service

1145200 L/Bdr. N. Cole,

'A' Troop,

'B' Battery,

9th Survey Regt. R.A.,

A.P.O. England.

12th June 1944.

Dear Mum and Dad,

Here I am at last, I guess you must have wondered what has been wrong seeing as how I have not written. You will naturally have guessed what the reason has been and you are right. The fact that there is no stamp and maybe the address (I can't find what it is until I've finished this letter) will tell you that I am "somewhere in France". Of course I still wont be able to tell you my exact whereabouts.

The sea voyage was to me as you know, a new experience, but luckily I wasn't seasick so was able to enjoy the trip. Anyway I am now all safe and sound on dry land.

There were a few funny incidents as we were leaving our point of embarkation. We were passing quite close to the shore for a while and passed one famous factory. They had a loudspeaker fixed up and as we were passing, they sent out "Transport ahoy, transport ahoy. Good luck and good hunting" You should have heard the replying cheer we sent up.

As we were on the roads making for the embarkation point, the people weren't half good to us. Every time we stopped they came dashing out with tea, lemonade, bread and jam, cigarettes, etc. it certainly was a smashing send off.

Just as the boat was pulling out, the people present were all shouting out and waving, etc. and twice we saw dear old ladies give a wave with their hankies and then dapping their eyes. I felt ever so sorry for them, goodness only knows what was passing through their minds.

At one place we were near to the coast and there were some railway engines, they all started blowing their whistles like mad, some doing the old 'dot, dot, dot, dash' sign.

In the last papers I saw there were some photos of the invasion fleet, etc., so you can guess what a wonderful sight it all was.

Well this might seem a bit of a jumble, but I have just written the things as I've remembered them.

Cheerio for this time then, I will write as soon as I've got the opportunity.

Much love,

Norman,

XXXXX

1145200 L/Bdr. N. Cole,

"A" Troop,

"B" Battery,

9th Survey Regt., R.A.,

A./P.O.,

A.E.F. France.

18th June, 1944.

Dear Mum and Dad,

First of all notice the change in our address. All the smokers were glad to get this one as it means they can have cigs. sent to them at duty free rates. I don't think I stand to gain anything. The last thing you will have received will be the field postcard that I sent to let you know that I was safe and sound. I have so far had a parcel sent off about the 5th. Containing the Torquay Times & Paignton News and the three letters sent on the 5th, 8th and 9th. What's more I have received a parcel from Mrs. Rhynd sending on some of Dundee's own cake. Boy ! It was good. Whilst on the question of food, don't ever get the idea that we are going short or living on bully & biscuits. We are getting really good tinned food. Breakfast usually consists of sausages and bacon, biscuits, marg. and jam. We have a light mid-day meal normally consisting of biscuits and jam again, occasionally though we manage a hot meal. We have our official hot meal in the evening and this is something like steak & kidney pudding, stewed steak, potatoes, mixed vegetables plus a desert of either duff or tinned fruit. I'll bet you didn't think we were living like that did you. Extra to all this we get a bar of chocolate and a fistful of hardboiled sweets. We have seen some papers out here the latest I've seen being the Daily Mirror of the 14th. I see they are giving you plenty of information & pictures of what's going on. I hope you're keeping all of them.

Yesterday there was a R.A.M.C. sergeant up here talking to us and we were talking about the different phases of the war. Whilst on the subject of Dunkirk he said "I was down in my hole once and the stuff was dropping all ways, suddenly I heard one that seemed to be coming straight for me I turned around and saw a worm coming through the end so I pulled him out and got right in its hole". We had quite a smile. I myself am now quite an expert at digging deep trenches in a very short time and also at taking headers into them without hurting myself. I was laid here in a trench about two days ago and heard someone reading a piece out of a paper on our life out here. It said that the boys had left their holes in the ground for the nearest barn. Grrrr!!! Words failed me!

Just a few yards along to my left now are nine little wooden crosses over the graves of some of the unlucky ones. The latest one, a sergeant was buried there about three days ago and last night I noticed that some of his pals had been out and scrounged some roses and placed them at the foot. Quite a touching sentiment I thought, in the midst of war.

Whilst I remember it, don't forget to let me know as soon as you get the voluntary allotment through & I shall know it's alright then.

Well I think this is about all for now so will finish. I will write again as soon as it's possible and in the meantime must write to Chrissie, Mrs. Rhynd and Betty.

Cheerio then.

All love.

Norman

XXXXX

I've just come back from a job to find thirteen letters awaiting me, and as several of them are yours, I'll answer them now.

Thanks very much for dealing with the parcel which Betty sent you. I've had several letters from her already so I know exactly what's happened from both sides of the journey.

Saying in your letter about the peas being in flower has just reminded me that we had fresh peas in our dinner today. Not far from here are some in a field going to waste so we are helping ourselves. The only sensible thing to do in the circumstances isn't it ?

I hope you keep Douglas posted up with my news as it's impossible to write to everyone here.

Now if Dad hasn't already bought a present, he had better get the signet ring. It doesn't matter if it does need more money. He has to buy it and there'll be trouble if he doesn't. The same goes for Mum, get what takes your fancy and take the money for it. The present has priority & cost is little or nothing.

I'll tell you anything of importance in the other letters in my next letter to you but will finish now.

Cheerio then,
Love,
Norman.
XXXX

Dear Mum & Dad,

Funny looking paper and envelope this isn't it. It's an issue to German troops on active service and as my paper isn't out at the moment this is quite useful.

I had a letter from Uncle George and Auntie yesterday which was quite unexpected.

Please do send on some prints of the film when you have the chance & I've just realised that one of them is a joke photo. Needless to say you will know which. I've just had a look at the photo I took of Dad indoors with his "spy glass" so I can quite imagine the hunt for the splinter in his finger. I'd like the chance to have one of your Cos lettuce but by the time I got it I'm afraid it wouldn't be edible.

Please send on the French-English dictionary as soon as you can as it will be extremely useful It's surprising what I can say in French already and there's plenty of scope for practice anyway.

I am going to try my hand at a little decorative needlework in a minute or two and if my efforts are at all good, you Mum will have a darn good souvenir of this blinking war & Dad also if I get an inspiration.

Well, I will write again soon.

Cheerio and Chins up.
Much love,
Norman.
XXXXXXX

Dear Mum & Dad,

I've got a supply of decent paper at last but it's from the same source - a present from the German Army.

The next pad isn't quite so good as this one but it is at least writing paper. Please send out a few envelopes in the next bundle of newspapers as these are what we are very short of.

I've got on very well so far with the souvenirs I'm making and they should look OK when they're finished. Apparently I can get some of the silk I require from a wee French lassie not far away.

Something strange has just occurred. I was looking around and was just going to write and say how peaceful it all looked, with cows in the fields, people walking along the road and all the corn rippling in the breeze. Before I could start it though a shell landed in the background and spoilt my fleeting idea.

I hope you are saving all the photos of this Second Front now as some of them I've seen in the papers sent out here will be very interesting indeed. I've seen quite a few photos of places I've been to and through. The scrapbook ran into two volumes before I joined up, so goodness only knows how many there will be by now.

It's very kind of Mr. Sutton to do what he has about this book, so please thank him for me. The best one as far as I can tell from the titles is "Weapons and Tactics" by Wintringham. Luckily it's the nearest one to the correct price too.

How is the Bankbook problem going on - have you heard any more ?

I spent an interesting hour yesterday watching a Jerry having a wash outdoors. Boy ! I bet he'd have been upset if he knew he'd been seen.

As far as I can tell I am getting every one of your letters. They usually arrive in bunches of about three now although in the early days I once had a bunch of thirteen to sort out. Not all of them were yours of course but quite a few were (Another shell just landed out there).

Whilst I am writing this, of course, Dad is in the middle of his three days holiday. I wonder what he's up to and I expect he's wondering the same about me, aren't you Pop ?

Got four chevrons have you Dad ? Well that beats me I've only got two. I never claimed any for my service in Civvie Street. You're senior soldier I suppose now, so what you say goes from now on !

I'm glad you all like the photos but if one of them is what I think- Phew ! I forgot all about it until I'd already sent it home.

This morning I was sat here in a little cubby hole on duty singing choruses for all I was worth. Can't you just imagine it. Also whistling over some of Mum's solos- "I have been alone" etc.

Thanks for the K.G.s photos.

There is just one thing I never told you and that was that on the journey over here I met a fellow who I was in the Torquay Boy's Brigade (Upton Vale) with me. He is now attached to (Here the word has been crossed out by the censor). I was lined up for my meal one day and thought I recognised his face, afterwards I went up to him and it was him alright. Strange wasn't it.

Yesterday I received your first letter in which you knew I was over here and by this time you should have had a few more... Don't worry about the other camera though it has not got lost in the post but is in safe custody.

You ask about the watch. It is still going darn well and keeping good time. It's had tons of dust blowing around it so when I get home I shall have to get it cleaned.

Well this is about the lot for now so I'll finish.

Cheerio, Much love.

Norman.

XXXXX

P.S. Another German envelope and don't be surprised if you get one with a reseal marked "Oi", "Name", "Ort", "Strasse"

(Letter censored by B Bennett)

130

I have quite a pile of your letters here to answer now, so here goes. I haven't been able to write before but, of course, as you will know that there are reasons. I hope I shall be able to write frequently again now.

I noticed in the papers that they have told you all about our Army Catering Corps baking a non staling bread. Well we have had some of this and it is extremely good believe me. Whilst on the topic of food, Therese my French lass was as pleased as punch the other evening because she had been given a little tea, and she and Andre (A great pal - French) decided they would give me a surprise and make me a cup of tea. They did this and it tasted lovely but there was one funny thing. The tea was made in a container similar to a basin and then strained into the teapot. The cups were filled to the brim from the teapot and the first quarter or so is drunk with the aid of a teaspoon. Afterwards they drink it from the cup in a normal way. I think this must be the usual way, at least around this part of France. Yesterday I had my photo taken several times and I hope one day you will see them.

I see very little of Welbe these days but as you have asked several times, I can say that he is quite well.

By a new regulation I can tell you certain things that have happened after a certain period of time has elapsed, so I might be able to tell you a few things of interest at last. Here are a few all over the allotted period.

One day we had built quite a decent cookhouse for our own use, with a tarpaulin roof, fireplace with oven, boiler, etc. We had a home-made table there from which the cooks served our meals. One day we heard a bomb coming down not very far away and not taking any risks we all dived for shelter. A big lump of mud landed clean through the cookhouse roof and missed all our meal by a few inches. We nearly had to have a meal of biscuits and cheese then, eh ?

Several places that we have been to have had very neat little graves at the roadside. It is very easy to tell German from British graves because the British graves have little crosses, white stone edgings, etc. and always plenty of flowers freshly replaced by the local inhabitants. I have yet to see a flower (other than weeds !) on a Bosche grave. This is quite understandable because a lot of what we've heard in the papers about them is true. Therese was punched in the chest when some of the Jerry were acting a bit brutal and she shouted something like "Celle Bosche" (Dirty Bosche) at them. Andre was slapped across the face twice in the street.

You ask in one of your letters how we get on for English news. We hear English news every day and we also get daily papers (about 2 days old)

Oh ! a good joke. We had all our girl friends for a camp fire sing-song one evening and they didn't half enjoy it. We sang English songs and they sang French and some tunes had words both in English and French. Anyway at the finish, Therese who is an amateur dramatic actress and singer said that I had a very good voice and that I ought to have it trained. What poor taste !!

Thanks very much for searching for the dictionary. I am learning a bit of conversational French and can get on fine now with the aid of a dictionary.

The books you sent me are reaching me quite safely and they are very much appreciated by my pals as well as myself. One chap gets the Listener every week so we have quite a selection.

I think this is about all for now so I will finish.

Cheerio and much love.

Norman

XXXXX

1145200 L/Bdr. N. Cole,

A' Troop,

'B' Battery,

9th Survey Regt. R.A.,

B.L.A.

21st July 1944.

Dear Mum & Dad,

Here I am at last with another letter. First of all please notice yet another change of address. Gets monotonous doesn't it?

I have spent a day in bed so far because in the early hours of this morning I had a bit of a bilious attack. It's not quite cleared off yet but not far from it.

One other important thing. If you haven't already got hold of a French - English dictionary don't bother now as I have been able to get one myself.

Now these questions you've been asking. I will once again answer them. There aren't half a lot of my letters going astray apparently.

The little camera is quite alright, my Post Bombardier had his wife to see him before we left England & she is holding it safely for me. It is quite alright.

The nice little bible you sent me has performed an act of war service. One day in our travels we came across a dead English soldier so naturally we decided to bury him. The short burial service was read from my bible.

You can take it from me that what Mr. Williams was writing about the French people is absolutely wrong. Every single person that I've spoken to about our bombing and shelling (and it's several) are sorry that French lives are lost but admit that it is and was very necessary. I've been in the company of some of them when drumfire barrages & heavy raids are in progress and they literally 'jump for joy'. A batch of Jerry prisoners were being marched along the road one day & he could hold himself no longer & lashed out at a couple of them The guard told him to stop as he would never help matters that way.

Thanks for sending on the writing paper and envelopes. It is very useful especially the envelopes. The books are always well and truly read through by everyone.

No Dad. Your thoughts were wrong this time. I was not at the service you heard broadcast from over here.

I have entered into a contract with one chap here. I do all his sewing (including making a sheath for a knife) and he does all my darning - we each prefer what the other hates. A good combination, eh ?

Well this is about all for now so I will finish.

Much love

Norman.

xxxx

xxxx

26th July 1944.

Dear Mum & Dad,

As you can see by what I'm writing on, your parcel has arrived safely, together with four letters.

I have also had a letter from Mrs. Rhynd, a parcel I mean.. It contained toothpaste, shaving soap, writing pad and envelopes. She also stresses in her letter that you are wanting to send out all the things I need but she will be ever so pleased if "I will let her send out a few things that I want."

At the present moment the sun is shining and I am sat at a little table stripped to the waist, writing this. Right beside me is a notice "Beware - booby traps" so I'm keeping my thieving hands to myself.

27th July 1944.

Dear Mum & Dad,

The parcel containing the French pocket book and pencils, etc. has reached me; it came yesterday evening as I expected. The French book is really smashing and by far the best of its kind that I've come across. It is so arranged that it can be used as a dictionary as well as for learning useful phrases. The pencils are of course for drawings and need these pencils to finish them off properly and of course to do any others that take my fancy. They're the next best thing to photographs for reviving memories..

Whilst mentioning photos, you'd be surprised at the collection there are in almost every house. They seem to do a great deal of their correspondence by view cards and the receivers keep them all in an album. I have just been looking at one collection which must have numbered about five hundred or so. Andre says that a very large amount of the people carry their cameras on Sunday walks, etc. It's not photography they're interested in but simply getting snapshots.

I am allowed to tell you certain incidents a fortnight after they have passed and as I have never yet mentioned any, I will recall a few in my next letters.

To start with, when we got here, as you know Cherbourg had not fallen so we were taken off our ship in a Tank Landing Craft drove towards the beaches until it grounded and we waited for the tide to go out so that we could step on to dry land. Whilst waiting there we could look out to sea and see the terrific armada of ships of all sorts and sizes. You will have seen photos in the papers.

We marched up to our area where we were to spend the night, passing between the German notices "Achtung Minen" - Beware Mines. Believe me we didn't stray off the beaten tracks at all. We slept in trenches. In the morning a shout went up "Monty". Everyone dashed to the road in time to see Mr. Churchill, Monty, Gen. Smuts, etc. travelling by in jeeps. We saw them return later on.

From this dispersal point we were send to spend the next night near one of our H.Qs. We started to dig in there, fairly late in the evening when the guard

reported movement in a nearby wood. Snipers had been there only hours previously so we soon got ourselves into the resemblance of a patrol but it turned out to be a straying cow. From this place we were deployed.

This deployment was in a small wood right in the midst of the infantry and beside some graves. Whilst we were there in fact, one English Sergeant was buried. It was a case of eight old graves, the new grave and then us. It was here that I learnt the art of diving in a trench as soon as we heard the 'Wheeow', 'Wheeow' of his 'Moaning Minnies' or 'Sobbing Sisters' (His mortars). I could flatten myself to about the height of a teacup - I'm sure of it. It was amusing to see the infantry prepare for their patrols into enemy lines. Black faces and hands, rubber shoes, soft caps, etc. and no unnecessary junk. I even heard an officer apologise because a patrol had been cancelled. Phew! If it had affected me I'd have jumped for joy. At this place we drew our water from a pump in a farmyard. Once we had a couple of fellows there when it was shelled, we spent an anxious few minutes looking for the first glimpse of them. They're OK.

Well, I'll make this the first instalment - more to follow. I don't intend to abuse the concession by mentioning place names, dates, names of troops, etc. but it will be of interest to you no doubt without all that.

Cheerio for this time then.

Much love

Norman.

XXXXX

Here I am at last with a letter. I have had a series of moves and it has been awkward for writing but it should be OK again now. I have quite a few of your letters to answer, so will look at them first.

I like the plans Mum is making for building a conservatory. I'll start on the plans and specification for the job and maybe Messrs. Vanstones will not get the job. What you suggest certainly sounds alright and we could do something like that and at the same time keep it from looking too common.

For goodness sake don't send on any Spanish magazines. It's bad enough trying to pick up French without starting on Spanish again.

You have got the wrong idea about Welbe and I not being together now. He has not been posted away but he is not on my post so I only see him when the H.Q. people and my post are anywhere together. I saw him only yesterday as a matter of fact and we were able to have a swim together. (In the sea too!) and it was really smashing. We are back at work now but nevertheless I've just had a swim. There is a swimming pool here quite near to us.

Now a little of the tale of our life out here, carrying on from where I left off. Remember I can give no names, places or times, etc.

From the position I told you about we advanced up to a certain building which you will quite probably unconsciously read about in the papers. One night I was on the roof there with my mate when shells started to fall almost on top of us. The scream of the shells was almost deafening so needless to say we quickly made our way into the building and safety. It was jet black. I woke up the others who were still asleep and got them moving down out the way. We went down a couple of flights of stairs and made for the centre of the building. We were groping around for an alcove that we knew existed when suddenly a shell dropped right beside us and all the glass came in and we were sprayed with water. Of course we thought the main had been burst. In the morning we found our mistake, someone had accidentally

knocked over a fire extinguisher. Did we laugh? There are things I can tell you about this position but not until after the war. We stayed a few days before moving and then we only moved about 300 yards. At this new place is where we made all our friends due mostly to the fact that we stayed for a considerable time (I will continue as soon as I can). We used to see them very frequently and in that way we learnt quite a bit of French.

When we were due to leave, we knew the evening before and all the girls came down quite early in the evening. It was about midnight when the revelry broke up. We were singing songs in English, some of which they knew in French, they were singing songs in French. Of course, we had to sing Land of Hope & Glory, Long, Long Trail and God Save the King The very last song was Auld Lang Syne (it has a French equivalent). Believe me there were tears that evening at the (as we thought) final farewell.

Therese and Andre made me absolutely promise to write to them. There is a sequel to these friends of ours that I cannot tell you about until the correct time has elapsed.

Whilst at this post we saw the 8000 ton raid on Caen and also the terrific artillery barrage that went with it.

At our new post we had a warmer reception, you would realise why if I could mention town names but on the other hand, we had a smashing air-raid shelter. One day I was out walking across the road when my sergeant shouted to me and with his arms indicated that enemy planes were approaching. They started machine gunning the road so I dived for a ditch. Lucky I did the bullets hit the road 3 ft in front of me. I think it was on that same day when I was looking at some houses that were almost to the ground, when a shot was fired at an officer behind me. It missed. We quickly got organised to search for the sniper and in all had a rifle (me), two sten guns and a revolver. We turned everywhere upside-down but couldn't find him. He didn't risk any more shots though when he saw we meant business.

One day whilst I was down in the cellar, I heard a strange sounding plane approaching and out of curiosity came up to see what it was. It turned out to be a flying bomb and dead over us its engine cut out. Of course it carried on for some way before touching the ground and exploding. They're no worse than bombs.

Well the end of the narrative for now and as the newspaper would put it - there is plenty of excitement in the next issue (When the time limit has expired).

I have just received five letters from you and will reply to them in my next letter.

Cheerio for now,

Much love,

Norman.

xxxxx

xxxxx

xxxxx

1st Sept. 1944.

Dear Mum & Dad,

Here is a letter which I'm certain you have been anxious to receive as at last I am able to tell you the names of places that I have been to & through.

If it bursts into pencil suddenly in the middle it will be because I have had an old pen nib given to me which is workable (just).

I've often pictured you trying to find out where I could possibly be stationed, so now at last you will be able to get the old gazetteer out and find out the sort of places I've been in - it will be an evening's amusement for you I guess. I cannot tell you right up to the present of course but its up to about a fortnight ago.

I left Cobham one fine summer's day and headed straight into the heart of London and down to the dock areas, districts which had suffered heavily from the blitz days as you know. Barbed wire enclosed camps had been built on the demolished house sites and into one of these we were accommodated. We were for security reasons confined to camp and the only time we could get out was to get to our car park, about half a mile distant, then only in organised marching parties.

In this area, of course, the dockers live and believe me they're generous to the extreme to troops. On our journey in, we had to go in slow easy stages when near the area owing to the great number of convoys on the move, and all the time there were jugs of tea, cakes, lemonade, cigarettes, etc. in plenty. It was obvious that everyone knew what was afoot, the person would be stupid that didn't realise.

As soon as we were installed in this camp, someone outside rigged up a loudspeaker from their wireless set to entertain us and let us hear the news bulletins. The camp's situation, Canning Town. I wont go into details of what we did, most of it was painting ship numbers, etc. on to the trucks but it wouldn't be very interesting to you. In these camps incidentally were large NAAFI's staffed by girl volunteers. They too for security reasons were unable to get outside the barbed wire. All our moving orders, and instructions for drawing 24 hr. rations, Mae

Wests, vomit bags (Yes! In case of seasickness in the ship's holds) etc., were given over mobile loudspeakers.

One day we had orders to move later in the day - it was cancelled. Later we were all lined up all ready to move to the docks - it was cancelled. Once we were even on the buses when (You're quite right!) - it was again cancelled. Eventually we did get to the docks, in buses, and were put on board a quite large cargo boat and we slept on palliases or else in hammocks, down in the holds, some of them even sleeping on deck. We had a cookhouse amidships & had quite good food the whole while. Whilst on this boat I met a fellow who used to be in the Boys' Brigade with me, quite a coincidence, eh?

On the journey we were told at one time that we were approaching the Straights of Dover and convoys were sometimes shelled. We were given abandon ship orders, fire orders, etc. by the captain speaking through a loudspeaker. Gosh we started to shiver in our shoes. Luckily for us a mist hid us and we got through unscathed. After a couple of days we awoke one morning to see we were steaming for land and for the most marvellous scene ever. Hundreds of ships of all sorts and sizes spread out as far as the eye could see. Warships steaming up and down the coast and occasionally a cruiser shelling the shore. No words could ever describe the scene & I guess pictures in the papers will have given you a little idea. The big ships were still and fussing around them were landing barges and speedboats, DUKWs, etc., all getting loads from the steamers and then disgorging them on to the beaches.

We landed in due course, marched to a field, whilst the officers got their instructions we snatched a short rest. We hadn't come far but we were in Assault Landing Order (carrying everything we owned) so we were tired. This was only the start and we had to march on for another mile or so before we reached our resting place for the night. It was here that we cooked and had our first meal from the 24 hrs ration packs. Each of these packs, incidentally, being small enough to fit in a mess tin and yet made three good meals each day. The first person we saw on landing was a French civvie standing watching us with a bicycle. From then to the time we reached our resting place we were all the time passing between "Achtung Minen" (Beware of Mines) signs which

Jerry hadn't had time to remove. The first village we hit was Graye sur Mer, about 300 yards from the beaches. From this point I have mentioned several little incidents in my previous serial letters so I will just supply the place names.

We spent our second night in a wood (Where we thought a sniper was about - it turned out to be a cow) not very far from Graye sur Mer. From there in the morning we made our way to St Aubin de Aquinas (? Spelling) and near here we were in a wood, our first work started (Here where Ron thought he saw the Jerries coming).

Our next move was to a water tower at Benouville and it was here that we made our French friends, girls and fellows from a nearby maternity home (Therese is the chemist there !!!) We were there quite a long time then into a field for a couple of day's rest. This was just after the fall of Caen, which we had been working preparing for and seen the results of our work in the terrific barrage of shells & the early morning bombardments. I thought France would crack in half. In these two days Caen was cleared up to the Canal, but Jerry was still the other side, so we deployed on the North West of Caen and did work for the eventual advance beyond. We came out for another day and then back to almost the same position. (It was here that I saw the flying bomb and had Jerry planes machine gunning, also where we couldn't find the sniper).

From here we went back to Benouville and were there for several days again, at the end of which we had our very emotional partings. I don't think I've told you about that though so here goes on the story (Not bored yet are you ?)

I didn't tell you any incidents during our second stay at Caen. Well there were none except one day seeing some people back looking at their damaged house - the two ladies about 45 crying their eyes out and yet not bitter towards us. Their house is past repair, it will have to be rebuilt. As I've already said, from here we went back to Benouville (Benouville of Calvados this is incidentally).

We knew the night before when we were leaving the tower so we were able to gather all our girl friends and Andre to another farewell singsong. In the morning I had to go out with a party to reel in telephone wire and it was almost time to depart when we got back. So off we dashed and they left their work and came down to the truck to see us off. There was a lot of promises to write, etc. and time was up. Bobby was saying goodbye to his Daisy (yes she was French) and me to my Therese She kissed me goodbye and then hurried away for about 12 yards and then turned into the hedge bitterly sobbing. She had to wait for Andre to escort her up. If I had gone to her it would only have prolonged the agony. I noticed Daisy had tears down her cheeks even before she turned away. They were good friends indeed. There were two fellows whose friends couldn't leave the hospital area so they went up for a quick goodbye. On their way to the truck they passed the returning Daisy, Therese and Andre, the two former still crying. It wasn't to be the end though as you will realise later. We had by this time driven Jerry from across the river and canal so we advanced to Honorine et Chauderette (Spelling might be a little askew). Here we were in an orchard surrounded by high trees (and also notices saying there were booby traps around). We had to dig in and make dugouts. Believe me they were lovely. Mine had cupboards built into one side, a gauze window and a mosquito proof doorway. The walls were lined with lead and we slept on chestnut paling covered with a thick mattress. This was rather a 'hot' spot but we thoroughly enjoyed it all. One day we were surprised to find the girls came up for a short visit on bicycles. It was here we kept our first lot of hens.

From Honorine we went through Caen to Cormelles where we worked for the eventual advance which closed the Falaise Pocket. It was here that I've had my most frightening experience which I wont and probably can't explain until I come home. It was here that we had a swimming pool available and had a building to both work and live in. I saw the tanks go in and come out at the end from this place. I cannot mention any place names after this so I will finish the story for a while. One town more that I know well owing to spending two day's rest there is Douvres les Deliverandes. I know Blainville, it being close to Benouville. I have been through Ouistreham. Had a swim in the sea at

Luc sur Mer & Lion sur Mer. Had a day's rest at Gazelle. Been several times to Mandeville (? Spelling) and through Bieville.

Well it's getting late now I'll finish off - any more towns that I think of that I know well and the ones I cannot mention yet, I'll tell you as soon as I can.

Cheerio for now then.

Much love,
Norman.
XXXX
XXXX
XXXX

Dear Mum & Dad,

Here I am at last. I know it's a long time ago but believe me it's not carelessness.

I will tell you why I haven't been able to write much or often for a short while although I mustn't tell you where this is happening - yet (After the permitted lapse I shall be able to). Incidents are also in this lapse order but I'm sure this one is permitted. I am stationed in quite a large house at the moment and extra to the normal duties I am doing medical treatment for the civilians. My clientele at the moment is from a fair sized village and dozens of spread out houses and farms. I've already told you that I do my normal duty at times that do not interfere with my clinic and then the real rush starts.

At ten-thirty in the morning until about twelve we are at it solid. We have dinner & then it starts again for an hour or so. Outside normal clinic hours there are of course always accidents and new patients. Only yesterday I had a bicycle accident case (sent to and kept in hospital) and two shrapnel cases. Busy little boy don't you think? Incidentally everyone comes up here and asks for "The Doctor" when they want to see me.

Well it's a quarter to ten now - clinic opens at ten-thirty, so I shall have to get washed and get my 'equipment' ready. Which am I, 'sawbones' or 'quack'?

Cheerio for now.
Much love,
Norman.
XXXX
XXXX
P.S. The photos have arrived alright but where are the ones taken with the little camera? Have you still got the negatives of them or has Ron's wife still got them?
N.J.C.

Dear Mum & Dad,

Here I am at last with a decent letter (I hope) after the fortnight's lapse I shall be able to tell you the reason why. I think I had better start this time by answering your letters.

I can quite understand the fact that several of those names were spelt wrong as I did it from memory and in any case some of the places are not much larger than villages.

It was an extremely good and to me original idea to hold a harvest festival in the school. That man is really wonderful isn't he !

The "Illustrated" that I wrote and asked you to save, you have already come by I see - well in it is a photo of Therese. On page eight the bottom left hand photo (interior of a church), Therese is the second from the right, and of course there are others that I know there. Those poor children will now be able to live in decent wards instead of in cellars all the time. Way back in those days (they seem to be months and months ago) I thought the fact that they could speak a little English was wonderful but I'm certain that I can get over far more French now than she could English then.

I and Ronald are on the tracks of the missing negatives and I hope to have something definite in a short time. Oh ! Before I forget it. Don't send the book out here to me, the "Illustrated" I mean.

An answer to another of your regular questions is needed in this letter. The farmyard stock was killed and eaten at least six week ago now.

Since the allotted period has elapsed, I can now tell you that we were in at the finishing off of the Le Havre pocket and this was one of our most exciting and interesting posts. Not long after we had got there, someone or other cut themselves a little so out came my first aid boxes, before long there was quite a number of both children and grown ups to have septic sores dressed. The malnutrition was very obvious here, as this particular very large house where we were was full of refugees from Le Havre itself, and almost without exception these children had these sores. Every day from then on, we had regular clinic starting at

10.30 a.m. and believe me, with someone helping, it took until about 12.00 to finish the lot. Besides this we were, of course, doing our normal jobs. One more thing before I finish the clinic subject. Our fame spread to a nearby village and we had people coming up from there, asking incidentally for the "Doctor", that was my nickname. I will tell you just a few of the cases out of interest. A man got a wound on his shoulder from a shell, he came up from the village. A mother brought up a little baby covered all over in sores,

I suspected eczema & sent him to a Red Cross station - it was. A cycle accident case who I took to hospital & she was detained for nearly a week. You will have read about the large daily bombardment that were given to flatten out a few of the very numerous block houses. We had a good view of this - I had my greatest satisfaction of the whole war here. At the height of one of the first big raids I saw a very heavy ack-ack battery open up, so needless to say I soon had their exact position sent through. Within about five minutes our artillery was firing airburst just over them. They didn't fire any more during that raid. I hope that several of them died like the cornered rats they were. In any case I bet the bomber crews were glad they stopped firing anyway. There are several interesting things that took place there which I can tell you easier than write about. We had a French chap living with us who spoke darn good English and he was waiting to be able to enter Le Havre. He was quite an asset as an interpreter and also as our chief bargainer. He, on one trip alone, managed to get us 17 eggs; we were very sorry indeed when we had to leave him. I'll tell you a little more about this place in one of my next letters.

For now I'll finish so Cheerio.

Cheerio for now.
Much love,
Norman.
XXXX
XXXX

7th October 1944.

Dear Mum & Dad,

I've got quite a few of your letters here in my pocket and I want to get them all answered up to date tonight but first of all a few items of interest.

My watch is going again now. One of my mates had a look at it & found out that the fault was negligible and had it right in about half a minute.

Now for a special item of interest to Dad. On my journey up here through Belgium I passed through the districts you were in at the last war. One place in particular was Albert because I was able to see the golden statue that you have told me about. It's on top of a large church or cathedral isn't it and there's large golden circles let into the roof just beneath it. It's right in the middle of the town isn't it and here's a street plan to see if you can picture it. (Here is drawn a plan of Arras town centre. A road from left to right with the church and shops above it. Then a road teeing into the top road, with shops either side.). One road was absolutely covered in the flags of the United Nations. I noticed some fair sized woods around there and I guess were a nuisance in the last war. Other places we came through were Cambrai and Mons. All around the district are last war cemeteries, some British, some Belgian, French or German. One quite nice one on the roadside had a sort of large marble gateway to it and on it was wording to the effect that the 7,662 officers and men who fell in the battle of Cambrai. Some number for one battle, eh? I've got a photograph of the golden statue which I'll keep until I come home, we've got somewhere in common to talk about now Dad. Believe me that photo (here part of letter torn away? By censor) a platform. What's more on a windy night they're draughty and on a shelling and bombing night I'm windy. It's very seldom we use those things though.

Well it's 9 p.m. now and I want to get in a good night's sleep so I'll finish now.

Cheerio and much love,

Norman.

10th October 1944.

Dear Mum & Dad,

By this time you should have received the letter where I told you about my journeys through Mons, Cambrai, Albert, etc. but I still haven't been able to send off my little parcel. It's more than patience you need in the army, it's endurance power.

The allotted period has elapsed since we arrived in Belgium first of all so I can tell you of a couple of interesting nights we spent. We landed up in a village named Baal, not a great distance south of Lier. We weren't lucky enough to get billets as is usual nowadays, so had to pitch our tent. This we did and immediately after tea attended a parade for changing French money into Belgian. Ron and I were the first two soldiers away from the area and also from the other troop which was even nearer the village. This meant that we were the first to set foot in there and just as we were entering two little girls came up to us and gave us a huge peach apiece. We wandered up through the main street until we saw two girls and an oldish fellow talking away. Just right wasn't it ? Two nice girls and a fellow obviously too old to be interested in them. We stopped and carried on a conversation in a mixture of French, English and Flemish. We might not have made ourselves understood very well but at least the party (many spectators by this time) when we were taken home for supper. We enjoyed this and before leaving they made us promise to come back the following evening when the local festival started. There was a fair in the village square and dancing & music all over the place, so next evening we duly turned up.

We had some lovely fruit tart for tea, bread & butter and coffee. There was a slight drizzle all the time and at this they were very annoyed as apparently they were wanting to have a snapshot of us.

The festivities followed which consisted on one blare of music of all kinds and everybody dancing around with everybody. Gosh, there's one funny incident here concerning the public conveniences out here but for the life of me I couldn't tell you it on paper. It would be far too long winded in describing to lose its funniness. I'll tell you all about it though plus an even worse incident when I get home.

Now to answer your letter.

The Harvest Festival in a school was at Homelands Central School and was conducted by Mr. Spaul. Gosh you sent the paper which contained all the details and I'm pretty certain you marked it so how on earth can you say you don't know anything about it.

The farmyard's cats and dog had no eating value so we left them for other troops to look after.

Well my tea's just about ready now so I must finish.

Cheerio & much love.
Norman.
XXXX
XXXX
XXXX

Dear Mum & Dad,

I had quite a letter writing 'do' about a week or so ago and my results have been to get letters from two people that I haven't heard from (or written to) since leaving England.

Thanks again for sending out the rebuilding plans but although I've criticised the scheme for Torhill Rd. I still can't find a decent alternative. This morning I had a paper & pencil out and set about designing but everything I did seemed even worse than the official design. Theirs looks too much like a Burtons" store for my liking. Mind you I think the blocks of flats are really smashing especially what they are fitting them up with - hot water, central heating, etc.

About Millie's present. As I've already said, take the money as you suggest & put it with yours. Do that definitely, then if I do manage to get something home myself so well & good, if not - well it just doesn't matter.

Still the Duty Free labels haven't arrived. Enough to try the patience of a Saint isn't it.

I think you'd better tell Millie that I've finished with her. I didn't think she would leave me for any other man. See how faithful I've been to her. It's a good job I'm not home or else she wouldn't half get her leg pulled.

You'll be getting cards and the like enclosed in your letters for weeks to come, there may also be an occasional drawing. I've got quite a large stock of various postcards so shall be sending home as many as possible each time.

There's not much interesting news to tell you nowadays as up to the time that I'm allowed to tell you details, things were pretty humdrum. We were very closely connected with a Church a short time ago and I made very great efforts to get a photo of the place. It was impossible. I got friendly with the local store man's daughter whilst there and on the day we left she gave me a lovely little pocket knife with a coloured photo of the church on its side. It's really a smashing little souvenir.

Incidentally we were the first troops to stop at this village so you can guess the welcome we got The people came crowding around. We got settled quite comfortably in a Drawing Room and was given the use of the kitchen, in a nearby house. Within a few minutes the kitchen table looked like a harvest festival. We had peaches, apples, tons of tomatoes, grapes and one oldish lady brought us down a bunch of flowers with tears in her eyes said it was for liberating her country. This same lady had tears in her eyes again when we were leaving their village. One day outside the house there was quite a sensation. The Maquis were marching a collaboratrix and a colaborator through the road to their local headquarters. Incidentally I passed through this village several times since & on one occasion a youth (perhaps about 22) was being marched up and down the main street by two Maquis. He had to hold a long pole on his left shoulder and give the Nazi salute with his right hand as he was being marched.

I'll tell you a few things about this village in my next letter but I've run out of paper until tomorrow.

Cheerio for now.
Much love.
Norman.
XXXX
XXXX
XXXX

Dear Mum & Dad,

I hope by this time that Dad's cold has gone. You've had it long enough now you know.

It's a pity we can't send home an unlimited amount of goods , at least not without Duty, or else I could easily have got you an alarm clock. The shops out here on the Marks & Spencer's lines have them piled up on the counters just like peacetime. There is also no shortage of wristwatches here at prices ranging from 600 francs (approx. £3.15.0) and pocket watches from about 550 francs (£2.10.0). Don't get the idea that because of this there are no shortages out here. Jerry couldn't work the systems as well as we did home. There are these luxuries out here but food is not plentiful, in England it was better no luxuries but ample food. Anyhow I expect Jerry ran the black market so it didn't pay him to organise things any other way.

Flash: I know a little boy in Northern France who killed two Germans by borrowing (without the owner's knowledge) a Gendarme's revolver. His age ? - about ten !

I'll tell you a thing that has made me smile out here occasionally & that is the way in which they advertise War Bonds for us to buy. They're nailed on roadside trees these notices. One reads "Buy a Bond to Bomb Berlin - Bye, bye Buy Bonds".

Another adaptation of this one is to put one part of the notice on one tree, the next about four trees further on, the next bit on again & so on. This one goes on three trees,

"Bye - Bye - Buy Bonds". This one goes on four trees, "Some like cognac - some prefer blondes - split the difference - &Buy Bonds". Another four tree one is "Buy Bonds - save dough - give the Hun - an extra blow." I think they're quite witty, don't you. There are other kinds of witty road signs "Go right or you'll go west".

An artificial grave on the roadside with the notice "This man didn't crawl along this track". Way back on the invasion coast of France I saw a signpost which said "Luc sur Mer 5 km, Las Deliverand 12 km, Ouistreham 14 km, London 349 km (The latter pointing out to sea.)

Bridges too have had some good names. I've been over these bridges out here, London Bridge, Tay Bridge, Forth Bridge, Winston Bridge, Churchill Bridge (Twin Bridges), Currant Bridge, Bubble Bridge, etc.

I see that Dad bought some officer's boots eh? Well you needn't expect me to salute you when I come home even if it is the clothes and not the man that we salute.

Well after all this time you will be pleased to hear that we have got our Duty Free labels, or to be more correct, some of us have (I know definitely that some units have had their second). Can't expect too much though, can we. I will now tell you what will be coming home in this parcel and to whom I would like you to send them for me. Incidentally there will be another thing for each of you in the near future.

Mum,	Scent, clogs brooch
Dad,	Cufflinks
Chrissie,	Scent & bracelet
Jean,	Bracelet.
Kath,	Scent
Mrs. Rhynd,	Medallion
Kay,	Scent.

For the Kirby grips I suggest Mum keeps two packets and send on two each to Jean, Kath and Chrissie. If you want any more of these I can send home any quantity you want. Of course Chrissie's, Jean's, Kath's, and Mrs Rhynd's gifts can all go in the same parcel with just a label or something to say which is which. You'll have to do this to let them know which is for which, because I'm not saying anything until I know they've received them.

Well this seems to be about all for now so I'll finish.

Cheerio,
Much love,
Norman.
XXXX
P.S. Be careful you don't get any soldiers after you when you've got the 'Soir de Paris' on.

12th November 1944.

Dear Mum & Dad,

I was surprised to see in your letter that Katy Perry's husband had been killed - I never knew she was married. How long ago was it? How on earth did you recognise her in the street. I'm certain I shouldn't know her now. It was years since I last saw her. I'm glad to know that Gordon Joy is still alright. Is he still a motor mechanic do you know or has he had to join up.

In the parcel which is on its way there is quite a considerable amount of postcards of all types and a booklet of views of Benouville Maternity Home. I hope you still have the press photos of the place, they show the cellars, etc. and this booklet shows the normal views. The girls took several photos of us against the 100 year old tree which I hope to get one day. It was against there that we used to jabber away to each other in our broken French & English.

Enclosed with this letter is a little sort of souvenir that I bought on Armistice Day in a NAAFI canteen. Now you've got entirely the wrong idea. In England I know a NAAFI is usually a wood or tin building with a rough and ready serving bar. Out here it is different. The NAAFI is the Grand Hotel taken over with all its staff & a smashing orchestra. Its an absolutely super Hotel. You go in, sit at a table & a waiter comes up and gets your order, what's more I should think there's a waiter to about every four or five tables. This is at Antwerp. There is another NAAFI the "Antwerp Arms". This is another large hotel with a huge bar lounge on the ground floor and a nice dining room with an all around balcony and - another nice orchestra. There is a YMCA in the Square, another large hotel but they've only taken over a part of it. The Salvation Army was the first one open and again they're in a terrific Hotel, really smart & modern. There is a NAAFI cinema and a NAAFI Theatre and it's in the latter that I've seen all the shows I've spoken about. All the stuff in my parcel was bought at this town, needless to say and I will be sending home view cards a couple at a time.

I'll finish the letter now but will tell you more about my doings in Antwerp in another letter

Cheerio for now then. Much love,

Norman

XXXX

29th November 1944.

(This is an incomplete letter - the early pages are missing)

Well this is all for now I think so I'll finish.

Oh! One thing I meant to tell you and that's about the children. Yesterday afternoon for instance I went out for a walk by myself. Almost continually there's kiddies running after you shouting "Hello Tommy" & then grabbing your hand and trotting at your side till the end of the street and then they say "Goodbye" and go back. Children will leave their mothers to touch your hand & say "Tommy" & then back to mother. Even children too young to walk alone will pull mother over until they can touch your hand. One lot yesterday beat the band, they had a carpet spread out on the ground and grabbed hold of me, so many that I couldn't get free and wanted me to sit down and sing with them. Actually I sat on a window sill & got them to sing a local song something like our "Yippee - yippee - I ". Then I said "I really must go".

Cheerio for now.
Much love,
Norman
XXXX
XXXX
XXXX

Dear Mum & Dad,

I am sat in a strange house writing this but can't as yet say where or why. Beside me a game of draughts is being played. - Dutch draughts of course. It is slightly different from the game that we always play. Pieces move forward in the usual way but an opponent's piece in an adjoining square behind can be taken by your piece jumping backwards over it. A "Queen" can move any number of squares in a straight line that it has been over. There is another variation they have started to play. One person has the white spaces on the back line alone occupied by men. The opponent has one piece only on the centre square on the back line. The one white piece has to get past the line of black pieces as they approach. All pieces move one move at a time. The piece trying to get through cannot jump over any piece but has to try to get past on empty squares.

A short while ago I had to do a rather important journey in one of my post trucks. By important I mean we weren't just gallivanting about. You'd never believe so much could happen to one vehicle in so short a time. A run of bad luck wasn't in it. To start with the water in the radiator started to steam so we stopped to find out what was wrong. We found that the pump which circulates the water was faulty. We decided to journey on slowly but the engine wouldn't start again. The petrol pump had gone "phut". We put that right and in doing so got an air-lock in the petrol pipes. We thought we'd had enough so decided to have a tow to the journey's end. Our troubles were not over though - the tow bar snapped in half. After much effort we got the engine ticking over slowly and started on our journey. I suppose we'd been going for about five minutes when the batteries stopped charging. We pulled up immediately and found water was pouring out of the radiator bottom. The fan belt had broken, opened a water tap and that meant that the batteries were not being charged. After all this we managed to get hold of a new belt and finish the journey. You wouldn't believe so much could happen in so short a time.

Well this is all I can write now as we've got to sing every few minutes "Hi, hi yippee" or "Tipperary".

Cheerio then.
Much love.
Norman.
xxxx
xxxx

P.S. Enclosing a 1 Guilder note (the type we printed for the Dutch Government). No next time ! This one is a genuine Dutch issue.

21st February 1945.

Dear Mum & Dad,

Please excuse this vary bad scribbling but I've just had a big shock. I was able this evening to get to Adri's house and on arrival here was told that the second younger brother had been killed by what I cannot yet say. Believe me these people here are every bit as family loving as you and Dad and the loss of this boy means the same to them as it would have been to you if it was me. Only last night I was in this very room playing with him so you can guess what a shock I had when this news greeted me. I have today written an application for permission to attend the funeral and will let you know if this is granted or not.

Please pass a message into the first church meeting that you attend and ask them all to pray for Mr. & Mrs. Van den Brekel & family - remember after all this time its like my own family. I shall be praying plenty for them myself

It is very difficult here for me as I can't speak to them enough to say all the things I'd like to.

Don't be surprised if I go rambling on for I feel that I will break down myself if I don't keep writing.

One thing their mother here is very pleased about is that they had that family photo taken only about a month ago. It's a smashing photo of him and they value it no end now. One of the embarrassing things that I had to do immediately I came in was to see the collection of all the photos in which he is featured.

I'm stopping for a second - I might or might not continue.

I've just had a look at a drawing of Christ wearing the crown of thorns and as soon as he had done it he told his mother to show it to me he was so proud of it. Both these boys would do anything to see me for a few minutes and used to cry when told I had to go away or if I was staying and they had to go to bed.

As a matter of fact only a minute or so before his death, he was asking his mother to give a shout immediately I arrived. He was hoping I'd turn up early in the afternoon instead of in the evening as normal.

It's the following morning that I am now writing this. It's easier to write now than it was sitting with mum on the point of collapse, Adri and Tonny breaking down occasionally and every so often a tear rolling down the cheek of both dad & Frans, the eldest brother. I should never have thought that a family of foreign nationality, with whom you can speak only a few broken sentences could get to mean so much to me.

Well this is all on that subject for now I think. I've got a couple of your letters here so I'll see what they have to say.

I was surprised to hear the news about Slades and I'm wondering what on earth Uncle Fred will do. I guess they're very worried.

I'm glad you've got hold of that book "Stand by to beach" and I'm quite keen to see what it covers. I imagine it will all be very familiar to me - it sounds like it anyhow.

This is all for now so I' finish off.

Much love,
Norman.
XXXX
XXXX
XXXX

P.S. - Fancy forgetting this - LEAVE ! As things stand at the moment my leave is due for Apl.3. However we've got such a poor allocation for leave in March that the Colonel is making enquiries. It may therefore be improved.

N.J.C.

25th Feb. 1945.

Dear Mum & Dad,

Once again I'm afraid this letter must be written in pencil - but what of it? Haven't got much time for all this 'must be in ink' nonsense. If it's bad manners then I'll be bad mannered when the pencil is most accessible.

Yesterday I was able to get to the house again with the express purpose of getting some undisturbed sleep - this was in the morning. In the afternoon, Tonny and her fiance took me along to the hospital to see Leo. Tomorrow he is to be buried but it is apparently the rule that the parents see him the day previous. Whilst we were there yesterday a Sister came and they intoned a prayer of some kind, so I presume that will happen again today when Mum & Dad's there. He was all prepared for this to take place - a little white sheet neatly folded so that only his hands and face were showing. Tonny was alright for a couple of minutes and then she broke down. She knelt on one knee beside the coffin, put her hand on his crossed hands and kept kissing him, quietly murmuring his name all the while. I'm rather glad I shall not be present when mum goes there today.

I can't for the life of me remember whether I told you the date of my leave or not, so to make sure I'll give it to you now. It's the 3rd of April. Just over a month so it's not too bad.

Yesterday I had a letter from Chrissie and she doesn't think the time is passing quickly enough. In the letter she says "I do hope it will be alright with your Mum. Should I write to her or what?"

You ought to drop her a line mum or dad because there's nothing like getting it from "the horse's mouth" is there! I mean this, I can tell her that you're looking forward to seeing her, but she doesn't know if I've any foundation for saying so - or not, does she?

My heart gives an extra thump or two, someone b---sh----gm (blancoing) for their leave. Boy I shall put more heart into that than

I should for any guard. It will be absolutely perfect if dad can manage his holidays (I almost said 'leave') at the same time. We shall be able to go places (including maybe North Bovey - what thinkest thou ?) I can't imagine many channel sailings being cancelled from now till my leave, so the date should be pretty accurate.

I'm glad you've been going to see Mrs. Kennard occasionally - I'll bet she really appreciates it.

Well this is about all for now

Cheerio then.

Much love,

Norman.

Dear Mum & dad,

I've just discovered this other letter in my writing pad so you must excuse its being delayed - it's my fault.

Yesterday I was able to go to Leo's funeral and as things are so very different to what they are in the funerals that I (and I think -you) have ever been to, I'll tell you something about it. To start with, two days after he was killed, they gave me a little printed card with his name, age, list of mourners, etc.

Yesterday morning I had to be at the house by quarter to nine in the morning. When I arrived there, there was only the family but very soon relatives started to arrive and at a quarter to ten we all set off for the church. In all seven people other than Leo were killed, so we had all the front pews in groups. The service which followed didn't mean very much to me as needless to say I couldn't understand the language and what's more I don't understand the Catholic form of funeral service. It was certainly very lovely though especially the singing. After the service the men only go to the cemetery and the women disperse to the house. In our particular cortege the order was this, first Leo's schoolmates, the hearse (drawn by a horse in a black coat) then us. Behind were the other hearses followed by their mourners. At the graveside the children sang some really lovely pieces. From the cemetery we walked back to the house, this time in pairs (it was single file before) where the ladies had coffee waiting for us. Slowly the relatives drifted away until just the normal ones were left.

There was one very pathetic incident. One very young boy or girl had been laid there with the others and behind was the mother, a person I should say about thirty years old. Whilst she could see the coffin she was alright but as they picked it up and carried it down through the aisle she started to shout out the name at the top of her voice and then just collapsed across the pew in front of her.

Well I think Leo's funeral is enough for this letter so I'll finish.

Cheerio.
Much love.
Norman.
xxxx

P.s. In the middle of the service we were all (the mourners) given another little card with all the names and dates of birth on one side- and a prayer on the other.

N.J.C.

Dear Mum & dad,

There is one thing I must tell you and that is an alteration in my leave date - OK it's not much. I said I should be home on the second but I was mistaken. I leave here on that date and my leave starts on the fourth (only 25 days now).

I received a nice long letter from Bern Symonds the other day, a really sensible one, telling me all about his troubles and what he is having to undergo for treatment. I also had one yesterday from Uncle George & Auntie Florrie.

I hope you are able to find those German books I was telling you about as they wont half be a help. We are still getting on with it alright.

I can tell you one little item of news. A little while back I spent almost a week on North Beveland, one of the islands off the West coast of Holland. The actual town I stayed in (there are only two) was Wissekerke. Out there the people are very fond of their national costume, you know, the white butterfly like hats for the ladies & the men with their baggy trousers. Even very young boys and girls are togged up in this quaint old dress. We were billeted in civvie houses, in pairs - Ron and I being in a farmhouse. A daughter there spoke a little English which helped a lot. The little bits of Dutch that we've picked up were not much use out there as they speak with an entirely different accent. I learnt one very interesting thing and that was how their famous hand-made lace is made. I will show you when I come home. There's no special equipment needed as you knit it on your fingers.

I was interested to hear that you can get grapefruit marmalade in England now. Be a pal and save a little bit until I come home - I think it's my favourite preserve (other than marrow preserve !).

Well now that you know my leave date, I hope your holidays can be made to fit in Dad. Don't forget to let me know as soon as you've got it all arranged.

You mention about flowers at Leo's funeral. There were none. His people being Catholics asked that people in place of flowers should give a mass for him. It amounts to this. You pay a certain amount to the Church, in this case about 5/3d to cover the choirboys expenses, etc. and then a service is held in his memory, a musical service. I'm enclosing with this letter the two cards concerning Leo's death. The one with all the names on is from the Church and the other is from Mum and Dad and concerns Leo alone. They have asked me to thank you for your letter & booklet you sent.

Also enclosed is one of the new one Guilder notes.

This all for now so Cheerio.

Much love.

Norman.

XXXX

XXXX

13th March 1945.

Dear Mum & Dad,

As ususal I seem to have several of your letters collected in my
pocket. There is one very funny incident that I must tell you about.
It concerns cook-Cole. Never knew that I'd been on a cook's course did
you - I haven't either but I had a 'do' at cooking the other day - mind
you, I didn't have much choice in the matter. The other morning we had a
bath parade and both the fellows who do our cooking normally, went on
it. It left myself and a signaller here to do the dinner, and believe me we
did 'do' it good & proper. There was meat to be roasted, that was o.k.,
tinned peas, that also o.k., but there were no potatoes to go with these other
things. At first we were in a proper stew & then we had a brainwave.
We would make dumplings. We got out all the ingredients that we
thought went into the making of dumplings & started mixing. Flour,
fat, a little milk, a pinch of both salt and baking powder and then a
little water for mixing purposes. After much kneading we rolled the
mixture into balls and put them into boiling water. At dinner time we
exspected them to have collapsed into look something like porridge. We
weren't half pleased when we saw that they were still in their original
shape. We tried them with a knife & ugh ! were they hard, the knife
almost broke in two. We didn't lose on the deal though, we sold them
to the local hockey club who were unable to get new balls.

I had intended to get this letter off to you yesterday but in the
morning I had to have some innoculations & for the rest of the day I
was done in. I'm not sure if the jabs were responsible or not, you see I
came back and played five strenuopus games of handball. I still feel
stiff all over.

Last night I received your letter saying that the German book should
have reached me, it hasn't as yet so presume it will by tonight's post.

Well, I'll finish now as I still far from being in a writing mood.

Cheerio then,
Much love,
Norman.
XXX

P.S. Dictionary arrived and is o.k. Thanks a lot.

Dear Mum & Dad,

I'm afraid this scribble is going to be even shorter than the last one. Anyhow I didn't expect to be able to write this one at all.

First of all, please send on the prints as soon as you can and keep the negatives at home. Do you think you could get some prints from the holiday snaps & send them on to Chrissie and of course for yourselves if you want them.

I received the tax-free label alright and once again, the first parcel.

Yesterday I was able to get into the town of Tilburg & the victory was being celebtrated here. In the morning was a youth procession just like ours at home, schools, scouts, etc. The afternoon was the time when the main event took place.

There was a large procession which was reviewed by Princess Juliana. When I got into the town square there were people on the Town Hall balcony but not the Princess.

She came out on to the balcony just before the procession arrived and boy did the people cheer. The band played the National Anthem and a couple of patriotic songs which the people sang with great gusto and then the procession started to go by. I had one of the best views possible as I had an uninterrupted view of both the Princess and the procession.. I had climbed up on to a large illumunated traffic sign.

(Here was a small sketch of the route of the procession) The procession took the route of the arrows and the princess was, as I've already said, on the Town Hall balcony.

In all during the day I was able to take fifteen photos of the celebrations.

Well I must finish now but will write again as soon as I can, but don't get worried if it's a week or so.

20th May 1945.

Dear Mum & Dad,

Well first of all I suppose you will notice that my letters wont be censored - that's finished with. I can now write and tell you exactly where I am and what I'm doing. We can even mention our locations on postcards, so you can see that it's right back to normal.

Now that we've got all these restrictions taken off, I'l start by telling you that I'm at present doing guards on the banks of the Maas - North of Tilburg. It's a bit different up here from what it used to be - I've seen thousands of bullets by night and mortars both day and night fly across here both ways.

Nowadays, of course, we aren't shooting at Germans but instead are stopping people from sneaking across the river from Northern Holland down here. The reason for all this is that in Northern Holland are thousands of Dutch SS Troops who know darn well that their number's up so in all probability several will try to get down here and pass off as ordinary civilians. We haven't got hold of any SS yet but have got some civvies. Three were caught yesterday. They came up the river on a barge - dived in for a swim then suddenly made for the shore. Earlier in the day a girl had been caught. She wanted our chaps to shoot her through the leg to make sure she wasn't returned.

I've just been in for a quiet swim in one of the canals here and feel quite cool now. I'm actually sitting on a grass bank writing this.

Tomorrow I get 24 hours rest back in Tilburg and then come up here for a further 48 hours. On Friday I spent a day in Antwerp and there's plenty to be bought there and not so many soldiers there. This last is a good thing as we can get into the canteens without queuing for ages now. I didn't do a lot of shopping this time but had a good look around. The V Bombs didn't do a great deal of damage to the shopping centre of Antwerp but I presume it must have done quite a fair amount in the whole of the city.

Whilst the V Bomb attacks were going on, we were not allowed into Antwerp and so for about three months we were not there. The first time we went in after the ban was lifted we backed the truck into a car park which was really a roped off street. We backed right on to a café in the window of which was a large notice "On demande une demoiselle", (A young lady on request). It reminded us of the difference between the Puritanical way of thinking here in Holland and the free thinking of Belgium.

Well it's my turn for guard now so I must finish.

Cheerio.
Much love.
Norman. XXXX

22/5/45.

Mum & Dad,

I'm off to Germany.

Norman.

Enclosed with this letter was a
Belgian 10 Franc banknote and a
Dutch two & a half Guilders banknote

22/5/45.

Dear Mum & Dad,

I'm off to Germany.

Cannot take money so here's a couple of souvenirs.

Love,

Norman.

With is latter letter was enclosed a ten franc French banknote,
a five franc and a ten franc Belgian banknotes,
and a two & a half "Zilverbon" Dutch banknote.

Undated letter but received 4th June 1945.

Now known to have been written on 1st June 1945.

Dear Mum & dad,

I've reached my destination at last - this is Germany and well into the interior. I can't tell you where I am, not because of security restrictions but because I don't know. You see we're in tents on a very large common and goodness only knows how far away the nearest village or town is, leave alone know its name. I do know this much, Hannover is not very far away. However let me start from the beginning and then give you the various impressions I've received on entering Germany and in the subsequent journey through the country.

On a Sunday morning I was out on a motor-bike arranging a football match for the next day between Fran's firm and my troop. When I got back to the camp it was to be greeted with the news that we were CB (confined to barracks) as we were moving off. What's more there was a spit & polish parade at 2 p.m. to say 'Goodbye' to our Brigadier (Corps. Commander R.A.). He told us that we were leaving 1st Corps. And going to Germany to work with an AA Brigade which is now really an Infantry Brigade. As there is no more technical work for us, we must all act as infantry - guards, etc.

We were allowed out of the school about eight o'clock and I made my way, needless to say, to Adri's house to spend my last few hours with them. They were all very sorry that I had go after knowing them for eight months. Mother said "We aren't half going to miss you in the evenings. About half past seven I shall look at the clock and say to Adri, Norman must be going to the NAAFI first before coming here "

When it came to saying Goodbye , Mum was alright until she had shake hands and then she just broke down. I guess they will miss the fun and games we used to have and I of course, am going to miss them an awful lot - and so to the actual journey up here.

The first day we went up through Nijmegan & Arnhem & up to a fair sized Durch town Enschede - a total journey of about 120 miles. Here in the evening Dickie and I went out to the NAAFI & for a stroll and saw things we haven't seen for ages, collaborators being rounded up, etc. just like the old days.

We put two Orange Soldiers on to a fight that had just broken out between two civvies and later had a long chat in the street to a man who had spent a lot of his life in the Dutch Indies.

Yesterday we started off again and within a quarter of an hour were passing into Germany.

On the way I made pencil notes on the margin of a Torquay Times of things that I noticed particularly and here they are:-

Osnabruck was the first large German city we came to & boy ! What a mess. It was somewhat reminiscent of Caen only just a shade better - there were a few houses standing in odd places. We went right through the main street and residential centres and it was just driving through a lane of debris for a lot of the way. There were quite a lot of people living there and some men were still working, pulling down unsafe walls and tidying up still further. It wasn't half a lovely sight to see Germans walking through their all but annihilated city, it must have let them know that their planes could never equal the damage that ours have done. Cheers for the RAF eh ? They did the work in Osnabrock alright.

Roads. I should imagine the Germans have destroyed utterly the main roads leading into the interior because I've never had such a nightmare journey in all my life. At times we wer travelling over tracks that it didn't seem possible get along, but slowly, painfully slowly, we made it. Sometimes we had to follow road deviations to a distance of about ten miles to cross a river about 100 yards across. I should imagine Jerry has kept his vital roads in good order and let the others look after themselves.

Hills. After being so long in Holland where the highest mountain is a hump back bridge, it was lovely to see hills getting ever nearer & nearer. When we got into this hilly countryside it looked just like England. Rugged lanes, just like Devon's and very pretty woods everywhere. It certainly is a very pretty country, in fact I'd say the prettiest (including England as a whole) I've ever seen.

Costume. I always thought that Tyrolean hats (complete with fuzzy brush) were an old national costume accessory and just worn on very special occasions My belief turned out to be a myth, I saw several men dressed in everyday clothing complete with a Tyrolean. The women's dress here is very nice & colourful and by far the most tasteful I've ever seen. Their frocks are usually of a brightly coloured floral design in which red, white and green seem to predominate. Another version is a plain coloured frock, usually white or something like pale blue with this bright material in the form of a little pinafore apron. There was one other fairly common type of dress and that was in the style of a gym-slip, usually a white blouse with either a pale blue or this flowered material as the slip. All this lovely dressing only tends to put the last little touch to the

Girls who certainly leave the rest of the continent standing for looks and attractiveness. The girls around here really are smashing and here is the first thing that the soldiers have got to resist.

Attitude of the civvies. They seem to have all different ideas of how they should react to us and we are getting absolute contrasts. The average person seems to watch us in a sort of passive manner, even the majority of the children just stand staring and saying and doing nothing as we pass by. I have even seen people weeping as our huge convoy passes along, I presume they are just thinking of Germany's hopeless position & disgrace of having thousands of troops pouring to tell you what you can & cannot do. On the other side of the picture there have been children waving and shouting to us and in one instance even giving the victory sign. I saw a mother holding up a little baby and getting him to wave to the Tommies. A very nice girl, perhaps about 20 years old, stood in a farmhouse door waving a duster to me, giving such a winsome smile.

At our first stop (we halt every two hours) an old boy walked down past us saying "Guten tag" to everyone. To all these things we've never even smiled but simply ignored them. To the children it is very hard & also to ignore the old man when he looks up into your face & passes the time of the day. It makes you feel so ignorant and ill mannered - however it's the only way to treat them yet a while I suppose.

Children. Two things struck me in particular about children, the first that they were almost all in bare feet (as were some of the grown-ups especially those working in the fields). The second was the fact that there is a lot o blondes amongst them.

Refugees. Several times I saw large rooms & halls that had been turned into temporary quarters for homeless people and on the roads were quite a lot of people pulling little handcarts or else on piled up horse drawn wagons, quite a lot had piles strapped on to bicycles which they were pushing if too loaded to ride.

Crops. Our road was all the time through the country & you'd never believe the terrific amount of cultivation here. We were for hundreds of miles on end passing huge corn, potato and vegetable fields. There seems to be enough corn here to make bread for the whole world. All the crops have lanes of tilled earth between each section. This was to prevent the entire crops being burnt if we dropped incendiaries on the fields. Jutting into these fields at very irregular intervals were Catholic wayside altars - it doesn't seem believable that the people who have committed all those dreadful atrocities could have a religion as well, does it.

Housing. The houses over here are very pretty indeed, I expect you've seen photos of German & Austrian houses. Several times we came across building estates in the course of construction. I never thought they could have had enough labour and materials to do this, but I'm, wrong.

The Occupation Troops I've seen so far all seem to have lovely billets, hotels and the like and are living in the conditions of privileged tourists. Mind you, the guards here are terrible, all this marching up and down, and standing at ease with eyes steady, sort of thing. I'm glad I don't have to do sentry duties.

I forgot to say that at one village early in our journey we came across was teeming with liberated Yugoslav prisoners of war and another was of Poles.

Here on this common we're living in our two man tents as it's only a two day's stay and we then move on to our occupation billets. Last night to crown it all I was on guard so was up and about early this morning. There's no water here for a wash and shave so I scooped some rainwater from the cab of my truck with a cup and poured into a wash bowl. Crude but effective, eh ?

Well this is enough for one letter I should think so I'll finish off.

Cheerio & much love.

Norman.

XXXX

2nd June 1945.

Dear Mum & Dad,

I am now in my final resting place in Germany, at least it's final until someone says "Come on Burma for you". Believe me or believe me not, I'm really thrilled with things out here.

To start with my room. Most of the fellows are billeted in larger rooms here in this lovely hotel and are therefore two or three to each room. I, on the contrary, the only one in the Battery, sleep alone in my own little nest. Let me give you a description of it. The size is about 12 ft x 9 ft, polished floor, papered walls and a panelled ceiling. There are two windows looking right over the main square. My bed is a very modern cream enamelled one with spring frame of course, a brand new mattress and a feather mattress on that (I've given away another feather tick I had). I'm using a down padded spread as a bolster, I've got to because the bed is so soft that my pillow alone just sinks into it. The pillow is what Mrs. Van den Brekel gave me. I have a white enamelled wash cabinet, another white enamelled locker, glass topped, and a glass case of shelves on which I keep my writing materials, books, etc. I've a little round table with red tablecloth, an armchair, a wall mirror, an electric heater minus element which with a bulb in I can use as a reading lamp.

My normal lamp is a real posh hanging bowl with the switch just over my head as I'm in bed. Well I don't think that's a bad set up, do you ?

Yesterday whilst looking at some German books I came across a lovely pigskin folder and it's just right for all my correspondence course papers, etc.

You will be wondering of course where all this is positioned, or in other words, where I am. The name of this village is Dassel and is 43 miles South of Hannover. It' quite a fair sized place and of course we are the only troops here. It is the most quaint place I've ever visited and is full of very old houses built of largely wood. All the houses here are like those old shops in Totnes.

The duties here are, of course, very heavy indeed. Guards come around about one in every three days. There are no cookhouse fatigues for the Gunners as we have some Polish men doing that. They were brought here as forced labour & as they can't get back to their country they do our work for food, cigarettes, etc. Eventually as we get things organised here, all our fatigues will be done by Germans, all the sweeping, window cleaning, laundering, etc.

These guards are a real 'spit & polish' 'do' needless to say, and it mounts in the Main Square - to impress the population.

As we can buy nothing here I shall be needing you to send me out a few things.

Writing paper (not envelopes at the moment as I've plenty) will be the most required article. Also I need a small tin of metal polish & a metal button stick. You'll know what I need here Dad, so I'll leave that one to you.

Well this is about all for now. Oh! No it isn't I've just remembered one thing. On our journey down here we actually came through Hannover and boy, what a mess. The damage started 9 kilometres (about five and a half miles) before Hannover itself and from 7 kilometres until we got right out of the city the other side I couldn't see one building that wasn't badly damaged. Almost the complete city is a ruin. I came to one huge block that looked o.k. but as we drew up to it, there was nothing behind the front wall but debris. The floors and back wall had collapsed to the ground. Hannover is literally no more.

Incidentally it's going to be fine for my studying here in this lovely quiet room all alone. Everywhere else you can hear voices or cookers or something.

Well this really must be the end so, Cheerio.

Much love.

Norman.

XXXX

P.S. Enclosed is a half mark (3d. Exact) & I will send on others when I get them - a 2 and a 5 mark notes at least.

Dear Mum & Dad,

I managed to get hold of a packet of German writing paper and this is it. Darn good isn't it.

Yesterday I was on guard and one of the many times I was turned out to interrogate civvies at the gate, I found two old ladies. Apparently one of the Russian forced labour workers here had been slightly drunk and had been threatening them. The house was all alone near a wood and as the telephones weren't working they were afraid he'd be back in the evening. The BSM and I (as his interpreter) went there and found that they lived with two old men, both cripples. We promised to send a patrol in that direction once or twice during the evening.

Today I am Billet NCO and therefore in charge of all today's fatigues, etc. Busy boy aren't I ?

Well it's ten minutes past teatime so I'll finish.

Cheerio,
Much love,
Norman.
XXXX
XXXX

Fear Mum & Dad,

Today I have sent off three parcels and there was another that went off about two days ago. In these are books of various kinds, some of which will not mean much to you as they are all German writing whereas others are very interesting as they're full of photos. Take a look in particular at the photo of the little boy in the second series of pictures in the Nuremburg book - the boy with a bayonet. You'll find it shakes you to see how early they started to install militarism into their young people. Another series gives the war in Poland. The reason for my suddenly sending these books is that we were due to move up to Hildersheim on Monday but the move had now been cancelled indefinitely.

When you look at the atlas I've sent you, the south of Hannover one, you'll find two maps that show Hannover quite large. Below there you'll find Hildersheim and then Dassel is further down & slightly left, in small print.

This morning here in the church we had a couple of weddings, I saw only one of them. The bride and bridegroom walk through the streets to the church and after the ceremony walk back the same way. The bloke had top hat and tails and the bride was in a white gown. The bridesmaids were in pink, and it looked very pretty indeed.

From now on, cameras & photography are officially allowed in the army, so I've no longer got to carry mine around in comparative secrecy.

I still don't know my leave date but hope it will be only about another month now.

You still keep writing about my getting out of the army & Vanstones. At the moment my getting out under any conditions in less than a year, is a very slim chance. What's more no firm's letters carry the slightest bit of influence.

Burma. The calls of men for Burma are so far few and far between. We have had about twenty men from the regiment so far. As the normal run of NCO's go my demob number is very high (44). This means that if any NCO's have to go from this troop, I shall be within the first couple. The obvious thing sounds to be at first hearing, to sling in stripes and get a better chance as a gunner. It doesn't work out that easy though. Even as a gunner my number would be very high and then again there's more of them than NCO's being called on. So far as I can see, it's better to keep my rank which would in all probability rise in a short time & take my chance like that than to take almost the same chance as a gunner and be posted as a gunner. Still, don't worry they haven't asked for me as yet & possibly never will.

Well just the few queries in your letters before I finish.

First my watch is perfect now.

Yes we get a lot of thunder showers here. I think it must be due to the high hills around us.

Our food is simply grand, we get rations like we did in England which is supplemented by butter & eggs which we can buy in large quantities.

I have got an envelope large enough for my Bank Book and I'll be sending it on one day when I'm in the mood.

Cheerio for now.

Jetz ist nicht lang vor ich om urlaub Zurich kommen.

Figure that one out if you can)

Love,
Norman
XXXX
XXXX

P.S. Enclosed is the route card we were given to come into Germany & also a German National Savings book.

Dear Mum & Dad,

Well it's been a couple of days since I've been able to write and this time it's because of a temporary move. We are now at a place called Sarstedt, between Hannover and Hildersheim As you can guess we've come up here for work & not the benefit of our health. An ammunition train was pulled into the station here, the day before yesterday & it caught fire. On it were 500 lb. bombs, landmines, etc., as well as tons of shells and smaller ammunition. Things started to happen in the form of three major explosions & hundreds of smaller ones. In the centre of the railway track was a crater like those Ten Ton Bess bombs make. There are the remains of the wagons blown for any distance up to half a mile. We're about that distance from the train , here in our factory home and there's a ten fool length of railway line just in the yard. There are some houses up to about two hundred yards away, completely destroyed and every one within about half a mile are seriously damaged. One oil-tanker wagon is blown right off the track & has landed about a hundred yards away in an allotment. There are still shells and mortar bombs littered all over the place so we're very careful where we step. It was in the middle of the night the first time I had to walk along the track & boy ! Was I pleased when I reached the road again.

Just behind our factory is a transit camp for Russians, Poles, Yugoslavs, Latvians, etc. I and another Lance Bombardier had to patrol their camp. They were moving off on their first stage and we had to make sure they didn't set fire to everything as they left. They hate the Germans so much that they are doing all the damage they can on their way out.

I've managed to get some photos of the train explosion & of the Russians waiting to move off and when I can, I'll send them on to you. Whilst on about photography - I've bought a new (second-hand) camera. It really is a lovely job for use in a studio or any kind of photos outdoors. I reckon it would cost at least about £12 in England now, whereas I got it for 50 marks (25/-) and 200 cigarettes (7/6d.). Not a bad deal eh ?

Well this is about all for now , so I'll say Cheerio.

Much love,
Norman.
xxxx
xxxx

21st June, 1945.

Dear Mum & Dad,

I've just done a full night's guard so you'll have to forgive me if I make more mistakes or if my writing is even more illegible that usual.

Seeing that we're living here in Sarstedt in a small group, the food is very much better. We're doing quite a lot of buying in the outlying farms and as a result we are having eggs for both breakfast and tea as well as a sprinkling in the salads made up from the lettuce, onions, etc . we get hold of. What's more, every morning the cooks find a bucket of fruit - cherries, gooseberries, red-currants & strawberries inside the cookhouse. The supply is 'ask no questions, told no lies'.

The factory here where we are billeted is called Voss Works and in peacetime they make electric & gas ranges, cooking utensils, etc., whereas now they have been making field kitchens, gun limbers, gun wheels, etc. A very large amount of slave labour was used here and for the housing there are several wooden hut camps right close by. Most are still occupied by Russians, Poles, Latvians, Lithuanians, Italians, etc. but not one very unsightly specimen. It is a sort of miniature concentration camp for Russian workers. It consists of two long wooden huts enclosed by barbed wire fences which have a sentry lane in them. The beds are double tier bunks and are packed so tight as to be almost touching. The space that all these people could walk about in, is roughly the size of our front garden. There was a notice saying they would be shot without warning if they acted suspiciously. One poor blighter had tried to make himself a comb out of a small piece of metal. Due to the lack of tools the teeth are about a quarter inch across. I've taken some photos and of course will in due time send them on.

Well I'm too tired to write any further so for now, Cheerio.

Much love,

Norman.

XXXX

Dear Mum & Dad,

Please excuse pencil for tonight. I've almost run out of ink so must buy some tomorrow. I expect a large bottle will cost about one & a half pence (or less).

First of all a little item of interest. I've just been reading a bit of a German book and came across this word (next line !)

Verschlussgeschwigdigkeiten and it means 'a quick grip wedge',

And another is

Schnappschlusseinstellungen - 'a snapshot holder'.

Nor for a very important thing. I've today sent away for particulars of a job in Ordnance Survey- this time in England. They have written to Survey Regiments to see if any surveyors were interested - this was about three weeks or so back. Four of our chaps applied but all later refused it and this why. They were all married men and the commencing pay is only £120 per year (about £2/5/- per week) & this isn't enough for them is it ?

Of course, it isn't much money but apparently they're trying to get it increased and in any case there are good prospects. It's not the start that matters, it's where you can finish up & govt. jobs of that type as you know are alright that way. Seeing as that my need for pocket money is so low each week and due to the fact that I shall have plenty of study to do & therefore not a lot of spare time for spending. Other than Govt. jobs, you're usually to pay a premium or else work for a couple of years with no pay, in order to finish up in a decent position.

To take my important Surveyors exams, I've got to be in an " approved office". That is an office in which already works a member of the Surveyor's Institute. That means a premium job. This Ord. Survey job will permit me to sit these exams which are the classic exams for surveyors and when I have passed and become an F.S.I (Fellow of the Surveyor's Institute) then it is easy to get a really good job.

As yet of course I know little about the job but when I get details, I'll let you know.

I was at the Divisional sports the other day and an officer asked three of us surveyors to do all the measuring required- long jumps, etc. The announcer

when he wanted us always asked for the three Gunner Surveyors. Once he saw me and noticed my stripes so as he grinned I said "Yeah. I'm getting annoyed at being demoted joking of course). So he announced over the loudhailers "There is one more alteration, this time not to the programme One of the surveyors is a Bombardier so it's 1 Bdr. and Gnrs.".

I've been to Brunswick today and bought some lenses and other equipment for my new camera & tomorrow we hope to take our first photo for the competition.

Well now it's 'lights out' so must finish.

Cheerio,

Much love,

Norman.

XXX

Letter undated.

Believed to have been written 22nd Oct. 1945

Dear Mum & Dad,

Well here I am back in Sarstedt & in bed, trying to work off the effects of the journey. It's been an education, political and humanitarian rather than a guard. The majority of it all I can only tell when I see you but Ill risk telling you of the return journey, a journey of emotions, fear, joy & sorrow. I'm sure you will never be able to get the atmosphere merely from this letter because even to me some of it seems more like a dream than anything else.

At five o'clock it was announced over the loudhailer system in our billet that all train guards with the exception of Bdr. Cole's and Bdr. Forbes' could leave camp. The two Bdrs. To report to the office for moving off instructions, and this we did and found we were to be transported to the station - Berlin Grunewald - at six o'clock that evening (Wednesday). This meant only an hour to get packed up & draw all our stores, rations, etc. so we got moving. In the rush we finished up with about twice the amount of rations we were entitled to which was a good start, especially as we had kept quite a lot of extra stuff from the forward journey, tins of tea, bully, etc.

We reached Grunewald at seven o'clock and moved in to railway coaches fitted out as bedrooms. These were alongside a platform, as was a cookhouse, dining hall, etc. all railway coaches converted and all a permanent fixture. It soon became apparent that although Bdr. Forbes' guard would be moving off somewhere about midnight, mine would be hanging around until the following mid-morning. We found a method of locking our carriage doors & so we were able to stroll around so long as we didn't wander too far. One of my chaps and I wandered about a civvies platform & got into conversation with a couple of girls who were waiting there, complete with rucksacks. It turned out that they, in common with hundreds of others were wanting to get into the British Zone, without having the necessary papers to do so. We decided that they were a couple of very decent girls, not the usual rif-raf that were trying to get through with English guards, so said they could travel with us. One girl had a friend there so she came with us also. We left them on the platform until things quietened down a bit and then whipped along to our coach and got them installed in the beds for a bit of sleep whilst we played cards to keep ourselves awake, just in case we were called out. At half past three we could keep awake no longer so decided to bed down. The beds were spring ones and I was sure that if I laid down beside the girl on my bed that she'd wake up, so the gentleman in me (yes there is just a little !!) came to the fore and I slept on the floor.

The civvies guard who travelled up to Berlin with us was very attracted to my guard and so I got permission for him to also do the return journey with us. In the morning we put the girls over in his coach because a R.E. officer daily inspected the rooms to see that the permanent staff were keeping them clean & I'm sure he wouldn't have approved.

At one o'clock our train was ready so we shifted all our kit over and on to our truck. The two R.E chaps who are in charge of the engine crew were the viscious bullying type and we started off with some arguments with them regarding which coach each was to travel in. When the railway guard brought the girls over these R.Es ticked him off and said that they'd see that no civvies did travel on our train. You see, although I was in charge of the whole train and it was my 'can to carry' who travelled and who didn't they only needed to drop a hint to their R.E officer for me to be put under close arrest. We hid the girls in an empty wagon when they weren't about and said we'd bring them forward at the first halt.

Eventually we moved off.

Our first halt was after only a few minutes travelling and of all places it was right bang in a main Berlin station, absolutely crowded with people wanting to travel our way. Immediately they started to pile into the open wagons so I sent the guard down to turf them all off (except our girls we'd put on). As a result people were almost fighting to get to me with papers and pleas to give them a lift, but only one had the necessary Russian permission and she, incidentally had lived in Torquay at some time or other. As she had the necessary permit I put her in the truck immediately behind mine, the only covered in one that was not occupied by us or the train crew. All around me was a surging mass of people pleading, some in German & some in English. One old lady was catching hold of my blouse, tears running down her face, pleading in German for a lift but it was no use. I daren't say 'yes' to one.

After about ten minutes we were still there and it was obviously impossible for three men to keep about three to four thousand people out of 67 trucks, so I said that people could travel to Magdeburg but that there they'd be turned off. Do you know, in a few seconds it was being announced over the station loudspeakers and you should have seen the rush. Just imagine it - over three thousand people in 67 open coal trucks - and there for a journey of a minimum of 15 hours - all through the night.

We fetched our girls down to the coach and the other two chaps who brought in one each & whilst we were stationary we got them hidden under our blankets.

Quite a lot of Russians were wanting to travel and they turned out some civvies from the covered truck behind ours and got in themselves. In a few seconds a Polish man came down with his wife "Some Russians have come into my truck and I am feared for my wife. You know that Russians are continually raping German & other women. Will one of you English soldiers please sleep with my wife and then all is well. He, like all other civvies over here, know that Englishmen have a sense of decency in them. Just imagine it for a moment, a man asking a stranger, but a stranger that he trusts, asking that his wife sleep with another man because he knows that if anything does happen, she at least wouldn't be brutally treated. You can put yourself in his place & know you'd do exactly the same yourself.

A Russian officer, a bit tipsy went up the bullying pair next door and wanted to travel in their van - as he asked he had his hand on a revolver. The bullies lost their bluster and asked me to deal with him. He travelled but not in one of our covered wagons !!

We move off.

We made another short halt a little later on before getting going in earnest. This time someone brought a little girl, about twelve years old, to ask if she could travel. They said her parents had been shot by the Russians and she was wanting to get to relations in the British Zone. We got her installed in the following waggon.

Incidentally, to help my story telling, my guards names were Bert, Sam & another Norman.

As I've already said our companions were all hand picked and therefore of the decent type.

Norman's and Sam's girls volunteered to be the cooks and we were glad of all our extra rations. We could cook the tins of food alright as the water they stood in didn't spill with the train rocking but the tea water was another tale. No matter how much we put in, by the time it was boiling there'd only be enough for about three or four mugs. Whenever possible we made our tea with boiling water drawn from the engine.

We had explained to the girls that for both their and our protection they must sleep in our beds and they said 'alright' they trusted us. It's a good job we did get so organised because about three in the morning, it was moonlight, about eleven Russians piled into our coach so I jumped out of bed and said "Anyone here speak English?" No answer. So "Spricht man Deutsch hier?" and this time an answer of "Ja". I explained that ours was the English train guard & he explained to the others and they started to get off. In the dim light the officer had seen the girls in bed and instead of raking them out he gave me a smile, as he thought, of understanding.

At Mardeburg nearly everyone got out but a few travelled on to Marienburg, the last station in the Russian Zone.

The dinner gong has just gone - I've plenty of work to do this afternoon & evening so I'll continue my story in my next letter - the frontier & rest of journey. Just like a serial story, eh?

Cheerio then.
Much love,
Norman.
XXXX

23rd October 1945

Dear Mum & Dad,

I suppose I'd better start off with the concluding incidents of the Berlin trip; so here goes.

The distance from Marienburg to the Zone Control was about six ot seven kilometres and for the last couple of these, our speed was about five miles a fortnight. Owing to the fact that we were travelling so slowly it seemed ages getting to the control and we were getting more & more jittery. Finally it came into sight and our worst fears were realised. It was obvious from the number of Russian soldiers, that they were going to search our train pretty thoroughly. Half a dozen squaddies went doubling back along the train to see if they could find anyone. I was stood in the doorway, cleaning my nails and pretending to look all innocent. I saw a Russian officer go into the coach in front of mine, the one the R.Es were travelling in so guessed he'd be in ours next. I looked around and found that the girls were pretending to be fast asleep. They were wearing our spare blouses and some had a cap laid on the pillow as if they'd been asleep with it on & it had dropped off. The Russian came up to me and said "are you carrying any civilians?" so I said "No. Of course not". "I must look to make sure he said" and climbed in. He made straight for my bed where Gerda was lying and gently pulled back the bedclothes from over her face, and one of my fellows said to him "Shh. Sleeping". He turned around and pointed to her curly hair so one of the chaps dashed over "Cigarettes" and gave him ten & I gave him two tins of bully and he grinned, turned round and walked out, saying "Ah it's good ja good".

Gerda was a brick scared as she was, she didn't bat an eyelid as he was lifting the bedclothes off from her face.

After about five more minutes we were given the signal to move off. The train started up & was just gathering a little speed when the Russians gave a Belgian & his wife permission to cross over into our Zone. They started to run for it and the girl had just got her hands on the floor of our wagon as she collapsed. Luckily we had a split second previously grabbed hold of her arms and were so able to haul her aboard. The husband got on alright. By the time we got to Helmstedt

191

she was a lot better - we'd learnt from the man that she was an expectant mother. We got her safely to a Red Cross station for treatment.

From Helmstedt to Brunswick the journey was very uneventful.

My first job on arrival was to hand in the consignment note to say that I'd brought back the train all complete and then, of course, to think about the next stage of the journey. I went back to our truck and the chaps said that another Bdr. had been to say that we had to get our kit out on to a nearby road where transport was going to meet us & take us to a transit camp. I went and saw this chap and told him that I wasn't going to lug my kit over about 20 railway lines & then only land up in a transit camp. I went along to the railwayman in charge of these sidings and told him that our truck had to be taken to Hannover. He understood alright and in due course an engine came & off we went. Apparently at Hannover station someone poked his head in the door and said "You'd better get everything out here and get on to another wagon or else you'll land up in a siding about 5 miles away. So the chap said "That's alright , we've got some sleep to make up".

At seven o'clock we saw the girls off on their various ways - we had all got to be such good friends that we were all very sorry when the time came to say "Goodbye".

From a nearby signal box I rang up the sidings R.T.O. and told him where we were and where we wanted to get to. Do you know in a short while an engine came up just for our one coach - we did feel honoured. We were taken down to the station sidings where we had about a 2 hour wait before being coupled up to a Sarstedt civvies train.

Through making our own way back, we were back a little before the others and we'd only had to lift out our kit a couple of yards from the time we left Berlin to the time we reached Sarstedt. Blow the army's official ways of doing things. It's far better to do your own.

Gerda lives at Cuxhaven and she has given me her address so that if I come home on leave that way I can call in to see her mother and father (Gerda will by then be back at work) She has also got both my army and home addresses so if when post with Germany is commenced, you get a letter through for me, you'll know who it's from.

I suppose you'll be telling Uncle Fred & Auntie Dot all about this journey, in fact I quite expect they'll be reading both these letters, so what will my Auntie say to my carryings on with another 'foreigner'. Tell Auntie that if I can find an English girl as nice as Gerda, in every way, I'll promise to marry her on the spot.

My name is on the list of people expected to be sent on leave in November, the 49th out of as list of just over 60. Needless to say as soon as I know the definite date, I'll be writing it to you.

This seems to be all for now, so Cheerio.

Much love.
Norman
XXXX
XXXX

2nd Nov. 1945.

Dear Mum & Dad,

Very important news to start with. My leave date is now the 12th of this month, this again being the date of actually leaving the regiment. One of our chaps who was due to go on the 12th wanted to go home on the 20th as his brother would then be home from the far east. We worked a swop for our mutual benefits. This should mean that I get home somewhere late the 14th or early the 15th.

Two nights ago I was out all night trying to ambush an armed raiding party that's operating in this area, we didn't see them but needless to say we shall keep on at it. Quite possibly we shall be out another couple of times before I leave on the 12th. You wouldn't know whether to laugh or cry if you could see us coming back, mud all over, tired out and absolutely like pirates to look at. Everyone dresses up just as he pleases. Personally I wear a woollen cap, a padded short coat with a hood, two pairs of trousers & two pairs of socks. In the interests of keeping warm we disregard appearances and look really scruffy. When the mud is added to this picture, plus the fact that we're bristling with arms - the perfect pirate scene is created. I always go out with rifle & bayonet, hand grenades stuffed in pockets & a lovely little dagger for close work. It's a German commando dagger & as sharp as a razor - Like to meet me one dark night ??

Yes I still hear very regularly from Tilburg & my short leave isn't coming quick enough for them. They've got one rabbit left & it's being kept to celebrate my return so they tell me.

This all for not I think.

Cheerio,
Much love,
Norman,
XXXX
XXXX

Dear Mum & Dad,

It's still very cold around these parts, if not so much so. It is now only 4 degrees below freezing point. It didn't snow all day yesterday or at all today so far and as a result the roads are a little better.

This morning I had to go out on a special detail. At half past nine a party of us went out to arrest three people who were wanted by the Field Security. The first one had been living in Chekoslovakia (?) for the past two years, the next was a prisoner in the American's hands and the third was at work. We tailed off after this bloke, so we instructed the two civvies police who were with us to find him and bring him to our camp and we came back. Later on two guards and myself had to take this chap to his home to collect washing kit, etc. and then whip him off to the Security Section. As soon as we got to his house his wife and his daughter flung their arms around his neck, crying their eyes out. There were also two old ladies crying away but not making such a 'to do'. The daughter would break away and say something then start howling again, fling her arms around his neck and start calling us swine. Of course, I could have arrested her on the spot for contempt of British soldiers but under the circumstances I pretended not to understand what she was saying.

Well I must pack up for now, so Cheerio'

Much love'
Norman.
XXXX
XXXX

P.S. This chap was the Burgomeister until we arrived & had done some work for the Gestapo.

Dear Mum & Dad,

Guess what ! I've got a gun, and when I say 'gun' I mean 'gun' not simply a rifle. It's a 25 pounder, complete with two ammunition limbers. When I first saw it I thought it was brand new but it' actually far from it. All the brasswork and bright steel is kept highly polished with metal polish so you can guess what it looks like. But wait a moment, this isn't all I've been given by far. In addition I've got a jeep, a half tracked armoured car and a quad (The vehicles used for towing guns).

In addition to all these material things I've got a gun crew of about fourteen or so men. Now you can see the sort of things I shall be getting up to for a while to come.

Another thing about our new life here. Rank in these Field Regts. Is considered more than in the old regiment. Just a couple of examples. We are not allowed to sleep in rooms where lower ranks sleep and we have a Mess of our own and daren't show foot inside the Gunner's Canteen. Sounds a bit snootiest I know, but remember these are an entirely different type of fellow here to the 9th and need a more disciplined life to keep them in order.

Yesterday I got hold of some views of this town and will be sending them on to you, possibly today. I've also got an original drawing of the main square here, done by a local artist of some renown and therefore worth about £5.0.0. I shall also be sending this on so please look after it for me. If it catches your fancy as a typical piece of Germany you can frame it. Frame it or store it, I don't mind which.

I think I mentioned that we have a smashing club here in the town, run by the regiment. It's complete with games rooms, library, lounge, dining lounge, reading and writing rooms, etc. quite a nice place in fact.

From my window here I can see the famous Herz Mountains where winter sports are held. (We have 175 prs. skis in the regiment !) Bad Hertzburg the famous winter resort isn't such a distance from here.

Before I forget it, could you please send out a writing pad for me to use in an emergency as we're told that it is very scarce around here.

Incidentally, we have to take down the old First Corps sign (Spearhead sign) and put up the 5th Div. sign (A 'Y' on a square background)

Well this is about all for now so will finish off. Don't send a packet of tea yet until I see what things work out like.

Cheerio then,
Much love.
Norman.
XXXX
XXXX

Within days of writing this last letter, I was recalled to England and demobilised

QUO FAS ET GLORIA DUCUNT

A MERRY CHRISTMAS

◀ Christmas card of 9th Survey
Regiment RA, sent to parents
Christmas 1944.

We roamed o'er Scotland's
                    mountains grand.
Old Irelands heights we did
                              survey.
And now from Englands
                    pleasant land
We Greet You on this
                    Christmas Day

9ᵗʰ SURVEY REGIMENT R.A.

▲ Christmas card of 9th Survey
Regiment RA, sent to parents
Christmas 1945.

Best Wishes for

CHRISTMAS

and the NEW YEAR

To Mum ~ Dad
With love
from Norman

B BATTERY R.A
9 SURVEY REGIMENT R.A.
B.L.A.